Basic Commerce Terms and Exercises

Stanley N Bartholomew FRSA

Edward Arnold

© Stanley N Bartholomew FRSA 1980

First published 1980
by Edward Arnold (Publishers) Ltd
41 Bedford Square London WC1B 3DQ

British Library Cataloguing in Publication Data
Bartholomew, Stanley Nicholas
    Basic commerce terms and exercises.
    1. Commerce—Terminology
    I. Title
    380'.01'4   HF1002

    ISBN 0-7131-0410-4

Printed in Great Britain by
Butler & Tanner Ltd, Frome and London

Contents

Acknowledgement

The publishers would like to thank the National Westminster Bank for the use of illustrations on pages 9, 29 and 30.

Preface

This book provides an introduction to Commerce for those who have little or no knowledge of the subject and as a revision and reference book for all students.

The book is made up of the following elements:

Commerce Terms

The author has concentrated on 196 basic Commerce Terms. These can be readily understood and will provide examination and non-examination students with basic knowledge of the subject. The Terms are divided into fifteen sections corresponding with the major divisions of the subject area. The core of all elementary Commerce syllabuses is covered.

Round 1 Questions

These may easily be answered by reference to the relevant Term indicated.

Round 2 Questions

These are a little more difficult and require a short essay-type answer. References to the relevant Term or Terms are again provided. Students should answer all Round 1 Questions on a particular topic before attempting Round 2 Questions.

Things to Do

These are graded 'jobs' which involve research. They will provide a basis for Commerce assignments.

Revision Tests

These are mixed tests referring to all the groups of Terms in the book. They include both Round 1 and Round 2 Questions.

Round 3 Questions

These are thirty-minute papers based on external examinations in Commerce. Marking schemes are provided, enabling students and teachers to assess performance.

The book will be useful for students taking CSE, RSA, GCE 'O' level and other elementary-Commerce examinations.

Sections Index

I
Banking

Banking Terms

Term

1 Banking

Banking is one of the Commercial Services or Aids to Trade. Try to remember the names of these by thinking of **WABIT**. This stands for *W*arehousing, *A*dvertising, *B*anking, *I*nsurance and *T*ransport.

2 Bank Services

Main services are current accounts, cheques, deposit accounts, savings accounts, budget accounts, bank Giro (credit transfers), loans, overdrafts, bank references, investments, safe deposits, night safes, cash dispenser machines, travellers' cheques, wills and executorship.

3 Bank Loan

A fixed sum borrowed for a fixed term at a fixed rate of interest.

4 Bank Overdraft

A short-term loan. A customer is allowed to overdraw his current account up to a fixed limit. Interest is charged on the overdrawn balance on a daily basis.

5 Commercial Banks

They offer banking services to the ordinary customer. Barclays Bank and the Midland Bank are examples of Commercial Banks.

6 Cheque

A form used by a customer for payments charged to his current account. You will find the picture of a specimen cheque on page 29.

7 Paying-in Slip

A form used by a customer for payments into his current account. You will find the picture of a specimen paying-in slip on page 29.

8 Current Account

An account into which individuals and firms pay money and from which they can withdraw money at any time. Interest is seldom allowed on credit balances.

9 Deposit Account

Interest is paid on the balance. Usually seven days' notice must be given to the bank if the customer wishes to withdraw part or all of his money. No overdrafts are allowed.

10 Specimen Signature Forms

Current account customers sign these so that the bank cashiers can verify the customers' cheque signatures.

11 Drawer

The person who has a bank current account and who signs his cheques.

12 Drawee

The bank at which the drawer keeps his current account and upon which his cheques are drawn. The bank will debit his account with the amounts of the cheques he issues.

13 Payee

The person named on the drawer's cheque as the one entitled to the amount stated on it.

14 General Crossing

A crossing is two parallel lines printed or written across a cheque.

0   19____   00-00-00

National Westminster Bank Limited
Anytown Branch
41 High Street, Anytown. Berks.

Pay _____ or order

£ _____

A SPECIMEN

⑈123456⑈ 00⑈0000⑈ 999999999⑈

A cheque crossed in this way must be paid into a bank account.

15 Special Crossing

A crossed cheque on which is written the name and branch of the payee's bank. This cheque can only be paid into that particular bank. A special crossing is the safest form of crossing.

9

16 Post-Dated Cheque
This has a date in the future on it; it cannot be paid into a banking account or cashed at a bank until the date is reached.

17 Stale Cheque
A cheque dated several months previously which the bank refuses to accept—it is usually marked 'out-of-date'.

18 Open cheque
One which is not crossed and can, therefore, be cashed at the drawer's bank.

19 Standing Order and Direct Debit
A Standing Order is a customer's instruction to a bank to make *regular, fixed* payments from his bank account.

A Direct Debit arrangement allows *varying* payments, at *irregular* intervals, to be made. For example, a supplier of goods sends a direct debit form for an agreed debt to the buyer's bank who will debit his account and arrange for the supplier's account to be credited.

20 Night Safe
A chute for customers to drop in a locked wallet containing money for the credit of their current accounts when the bank is closed.

21 Cash Dispenser Machine
A customer can withdraw cash up to a fixed amount from his bank after closing time by inserting his cash card in this machine.

22 Savings Account
Small metal safes are supplied by a bank for small savings at home. Interest is paid on the contents when they are deposited with the bank, and withdrawals are easily arranged.

23 Bank Statement
A copy of a customer's banking account, showing his debits (amounts withdrawn), his credits (amounts paid in), and the daily balances of his current account. Look at the picture of a specimen bank statement on page 30.

24 'In the Red'
It means that a customer has a bank overdraft (authorized or unauthorized). Before computerization overdrawn balances were shown in red on bank statements.

25 Banks' Clearing Houses
The commercial banks in co-operation with the Bank of England provide 'meeting places' in London and other main cities where millions of cheques which are drawn each day are sorted out by computers and debited or credited to the various banks. They are then returned to the drawee banks for debiting to their own customers' current accounts.

26 Bank of England

It is the central bank of England and Wales and controls the issue of bank notes. It is the Government's bank and it looks after the country's gold reserves. It is the commercial bankers' bank. It has an important part to play in carrying out the country's monetary policy.

27 Merchant Banks

They are specialized banks which mainly deal in the short-term money market and the capital market. Foreign exchange dealings form a very important part of their business.

28 Credit Cards

Commercial banks can issue customers holding current accounts a credit card to replace cash up to a fixed amount when they shop, stay in hotels, etc. Also, it replaces the cheque which in many shops, etc, will not be accepted in exchange for goods and services. Access and Barclaycard are examples of credit cards.

29 Cheque Card

Commercial banks can issue customers holding current accounts a cheque card to guarantee a customer's cheque. It identifies him by a serial number and his signature and guarantees his cheque up to a fixed amount. With this card, he can withdraw cash from any bank up to the fixed amount.

30 Bank Giro

This is a means of transferring money through the Commercial Banks (see terms 5 and 2). The time and expense of writing and posting cheques is saved. The debtor fills in a Bank Giro Credit form for each payment and hands it to his bank. The bank debits his account and transfers the amount of money to the creditors' banks. Although the creditor must have a bank current account to receive credits, the debtor need not possess one but he will need to pay any bank he uses a small fee for the service.

An employer can, for example, give his bank one cheque for the total wages bill and the bank will arrange all the credits to the employees' current accounts with other banks. For a small fee, any person can take the cash and a bill, his gas account, for example, to any bank and arrange a credit transfer to the current account of the Gas Board. The system is also useful when a customer wishes to pay money into his current account but is unable to visit his own branch.

Round 1 Questions on Banking

Check your answers by reference to the Term number shown in brackets at the end of each question.

1 Banking is one of the Commercial Services or Aids to Trade. How many such services are there? (1)

2 Write down 5 of the main banking services. **(2)**

3 A fixed sum borrowed from a bank for a fixed period at a fixed rate of interest is known as a ... . **(3)**

4 A short-term loan upon which a bank charges interest on a daily basis is called a ... . **(4)**

5 Your salary of £200 is due at the end of the month (eight days' time). You wish to buy immediately an article in a sale for £50. Which type of bank loan would be the cheaper one for you? **(4)**

6 The 15 banking services in the list are offered by the ... banks. **(5)**

7 A customer fills in a ... - ... ... to place money in his bank current account. **(7)**

8 A customer uses a ... to withdraw money from his bank current account. **(6)**

9 Interest is seldom allowed by banks to customers who have credit in their ... accounts. **(8)**

10 If a customer leaves money in a bank and agrees to give about seven days' notice of withdrawal of part or all of it, he will earn interest on the credit balance of his ... account. **(9)**

11 A bank cashier can verify a customer's signature by reference to his ... ... **(10)**

12 The three parties to a cheque are (a) ... , the person who signs it, (b) ... , the bank upon which it is drawn, and (c) ... , the person named on it as the one entitled to the amount stated. **(11–13)**

13 A cheque with two parallel lines across it must be paid into a bank. The safest form of cheque has the name and branch of the payee's bank written between the lines. It has a ... crossing. **(15)**

14 The cheque described in Question 13 but without the payee's bank named in the crossing has a ... crossing. **(14)**

15 If a cheque has a date in the future on it, we call it a ... - ... . **(16)**

16 A cheque dated several months previously will not be accepted by a bank because it is ... ... It is known as a ... . **(17)**

17 If a bank customer wishes to draw cash from his account or allow somebody else to do so, he uses an ... cheque. **(18)**

18 Susan buys some furniture, costing £200, on credit. The shop-keeper agrees to accept £20 per month for 10 months. Susan instructs her bank to pay the retailer's bank the regular sum by giving her bank a ... . **(19)**

19 Shop-keepers do not like to keep large sums of money on the premises after the banks have closed. So, many of them pay cash and cheques into their bank by means of the ... . **(20)**

20 A bank customer can withdraw small sums of cash from his bank after closing time by using the ... ... (21)
21 Interest is paid by a bank on money taken from small metal safes kept at a person's home if the cash is placed in a bank's ... . (22)
22 A customer receives at fairly regular intervals, or on request, a copy of his bank current account. This document is known as a ... . (23)
23 'In the red' means that a customer has a ... ... and has taken out of his bank current account more than he has in it. (24)
24 The 'meeting places' where the commercial banks deal with each others' cheques by means of computers and debit and credit each others' accounts with them are known as ... ... They co-operate with the ... ... at these 'meeting places'. (25)
25 The Government's bank is known as the ... ... (26)
26 The banks which specialize in the short-term money market, the capital market, and foreign exchange dealings are called ... . (27)
27 A ... card replaces the use of cash up to a fixed sum. (28)
28 A ... card guarantees a bank customer's cheque. (29)
29 A bank customer can obtain cash up to a fixed amount from any bank if he produces his ... . (29)
30 The bank credit transfer system is known as ... ... and it can also be used by a customer to pay money into his bank current account whilst he is away from home. (30)

Things to do in your Banking Research and Studies

1 Visit several banks to obtain literature about bank accounts and banking services.
2 Copy out and fill in several paying-in slips from page 29.
3 Copy out and fill in several cheques, some crossed, others un-crossed, from page 9.
4 Copy out and fill in a Bank Statement from page 30, using all your paying-in slips and cheques for this purpose; show your credit or debit balance each time you fill in an amount.
5 Draw a street plan of a local town, large enough to show the positions of various businesses and services. Show the position of the bank or banks.
6 Inquire about the main services given by the banks locally to industrialists, commercial businesses, direct service businesses (local council, doctors, dentists, solicitors, teachers, etc), and to the consumer (people who buy goods and services).

Round 2 Questions on Banking

Check your answer by reference to the Term number shown in brackets at the end of each question.

1 Explain the terms 'bank loan' and 'bank overdraft'. **(3–4)**
2 List the main purposes of (a) bank current accounts and (b) bank deposit accounts. State some of the advantages in having both types of account. **(8–9)**
3 John has a bank current account. State (a) how he normally increases his bank balance, (b) how he usually draws amounts from it for himself and others, and (c) what written evidence he can obtain to show what has happened to his money during any given period of time. **(6, 7, 23)**
4 Explain the reasons for using 'open' cheques, cheques with a general crossing, and cheques with a special crossing. **(14, 15, 18)**
5 Explain the meaning of the terms 'standing order' and 'direct debit'. **(19)**
6 What methods are available to customers who wish to (a) pay money into their bank and (b) withdraw small sums from their bank when their banks are closed? **(20–21)**
7 For what purpose are small metal safes supplied by banks? **(22)**
8 Describe the functions of the Banks' Clearing Houses. **(25)**
9 List the functions of the Bank of England. **(25–26)**
10 In what types of banking do merchant bankers specialize? **(27)**
11 What are the main differences between credit cards and cheque cards? **(28–29)**
12 How can a business firm make use of the Bank Giro system? Explain briefly how the system works. **(30)**

2

Insurance

Insurance Terms

Term

31 **Purpose of Insurance**
To lessen the risk of financial worry and loss.

32 **Risk**
The chance or hazard of a business or personal financial loss.

33 **Assurance**
Life insurance.

34 **Assured**
A person who takes out a life assurance policy to insure against certain risks.

35 **Insurers**
They undertake insurance business and include Insurance Companies, Underwriters, Friendly Societies, Trade Unions, the Post Office, and the Government (six main groups).

36 **Insured**
A person who is insured against a risk and is a party to the insurance policy.

37 **Proposal Form**
The application form for insurance which a person fills in and sends to an insurer.

38 **Utmost Good Faith**
The insurers take on the risk on the understanding that the person filling in the proposal form has given full details to enable the insurers to assess the risk they are taking on. The insurers, too, must word the policy in clear, understandable terms.

39 **Policy**
The insurance contract giving the terms and conditions in detail.

40 **Cover Note**
A letter or form from the insurer to inform the insured that he is covered by insurance immediately and that his policy will arrive later.

41 Premium
The amount paid (usually annually) by the insured to the insurer to keep the policy 'alive'.

42 Renewal Notice
A letter or form from the insurer reminding the insured that the next premium is due if he wishes to renew his policy.

43 Days of Grace
The extra days allowed by the insurer for the insured to renew his policy (usually 15 days for insurance and 30 days for life assurance).

44 Insurable Risks
The main types of insurance are Life Assurance, Goods in Transit, Fire, Theft and Burglary, Shop Windows, Motor Insurance, Employers' Liability, Public Liability, Accident and Sickness, Unemployment, Householders' policies to cover an insured's house and its contents including Comprehensive Insurance policies, part of a firm's Bad Debts, Cash in Transit, Fidelity Guarantee, Personal Liability, Mortgage Protection, Marine and Aviation Insurance.

45 Insurable Interest
The insured must suffer some kind of loss before being entitled to claim against the insurer. You are only allowed to insure against something happening if you are going to lose when it happens.

46 Uninsurable Risks
There are some risks which cannot be insured. Normally the insurer is able to assess the size of the premium by the number of times that a particular event has occurred in a particular set of circumstances, over a past number of years. If an event is not so measurable, then it is uninsurable. Gambling is a good example of an uninsurable risk—a person cannot insure against a horse losing a race.

47 Third Party Insurance
It is a compulsory motor insurance against claims made by the injured party against the motorist for damage to himself or his property.

48 Pooling of Risk
Millions of people pay insurance premiums into a 'pool' out of which any claims they make are paid.

49 Indemnity
Protection against loss. This puts you back in the position you were before your loss happened. You should not make a profit out of the compensation.

50 Underwriters
Individuals who are insurers—they usually meet at Lloyd's and group together to form syndicates to share large risks such as the loss of an oil-rig or a liner.

51 Lloyd's

A market place where underwriters and insurance brokers meet to carry out insurance business. It is an international market for most types of insurance, particularly marine insurance.

52 Types of Insurance Cover

Note the main types listed under Term 44 above.

53 Principles of Insurance

These are the 'rules' of insurance. There are three main rules—utmost good faith, insurable interest, and indemnity.

Round 1 Questions on Insurance

Check your answers by reference to the Term number shown in brackets at the end of each question.

31 The purpose of insurance is to lessen the ... of ... worry and loss. **(31)**

32 The chance or hazard of financial loss is known in insurance as a .... . **(32)**

33 Life assurance, which can be (a) Whole Life—payable at death of the insured person—or (b) Endowment—payable at death or after a fixed number of years—is known as .... . **(33)**

34 A person who takes out a life assurance policy is called the .... . **(34)**

35 The companies which issue insurance policies to those wishing to be insured are called ... . **(35)**

36 List the main groups which undertake insurance business. **(35)**

37 A person who is insured against a risk is known as the ... . **(36)**

38 The application form for insurance is called a ... . **(37)**

39 Insurers undertake an insurance risk on the understanding that the insured has given full details about himself and the risk in his proposal form and the insurers must word the policy in clear, understandable terms. These understandings form one of the principles of insurance known as ... ... **(38)**

40 The insurance policy is a contract giving the ... and ... in detail. **(39)**

41 An insurance cover note means that the insured is ... by insurance ... and that his ... will arrive later. **(40)**

42 The amount paid by the insured to the insurer to keep a policy 'alive' is known as the ... . **(41)**

43 When the next ... is due to keep the policy 'alive' the insured will receive a ... ... from the insurer. **(41–42)**

44 What do you understand by the use of the term 'Days of Grace'? **(43)**

45 List as many of the main types of insurable risks as you can recall. **(44)**

46 If a person owns a house and wishes to insure against loss through fire, he has an ... . **(45)**

47 If John bets on a horse winning a certain race, he cannot insure against that risk because it is an ... risk. **(46)**

48 The compulsory motor insurance which must be taken out by motorists to cover injuries to pedestrians and damage to other people's property is termed ... ... insurance. **(47)**

49 An insurance company places the insurance premiums it collects in a '...' out of which claims are paid. This safeguard is known as the '... of risk'. **(48)**

50 Indemnity means ... ... **(49)**

51 The individuals who meet at Lloyd's to insure heavy risks are known as ... . **(50)**

52 Lloyd's is a ... ... where its ... and ... ... meet. **(51)**

53 'Utmost good faith', 'insurable interest' and 'indemnity' are three ... of ... . These are the ... of insurance. **(53)**

Things to do in your Insurance Research and Studies

7 Discuss the type of insurance cover you would need if you owned a house or flat and ran a car.

8 Discuss the types of insurance cover to be considered if you owned shop premises and sold goods.

9 Find out all you can about Lloyd's of London, underwriters, and the Lutine Bell.

10 On your street plan (suggested on page 13, number 5) add the location of insurance people in your town. Include the Department of Health and Social Security who deal with National Insurance.

11 Find out about the work of Insurance Companies, Insurance Brokers, Friendly Societies, and Underwriters. Also find out what Actuaries and Assessors do in the business of insurance.

12 Collect a few Proposal Forms and other insurance papers and documents for discussion.

Round 2 Questions on Insurance

Check your answers by reference to the Term number shown in brackets at the end of each question.

13 What insurance business has been transacted before an insured person receives a cover note from his insurer? **(37, 40, 41)**

14 Three principles of insurance are 'utmost good faith', 'insurable interest' and 'indemnity'. Explain these three 'rules'. (38, 45, 49, 53)

15 Explain the meanings of 'renewal notice' and 'days of grace'. (42–43)

16 What do you understand by the term 'third party' insurance, and why is it compulsory for motorists? (47)

17 What systems do insurance businesses use to make sure that they can meet large insurance claims? (48, 50)

18 Give one example of an 'insurable risk' and one example of an 'uninsurable risk', and explain the two terms. (44–46)

3
Transport

Transport Terms

Term

54 Transport
The conveyance of passengers, animals and goods from place to place.

55 Types of Transport
The main kinds are walking, cycling, motor-cycling, motoring, motor-vans, motor lorries, horses, tractors, buses, trams, taxis, coaches, goods trains, freight-liners, passenger trains, express freight trains, various types of small boats, ferries, canal barges, liners, tramp steamers, tankers, coastal steamers, hovercraft, air-liners, charter-planes, chair-lifts, pipe-lines.

56 Transport Divisions
There are two divisions—passenger transport and goods transport.

57 Transport Classification
There are five types: Inland waterways (canal, lake, river), road, rail, sea and air.

58 Transport ownership
It is owned by three groups. They are private individuals, private firms (called private enterprise) and public enterprises (state-owned and owned by local councils or area authorities).

59 Private Transport
Means of transport owned by private individuals.

60 Private Enterprise Transport
Means of transport owned by private firms.

61 Public Transport
The public, through their Government, local councils and local area authorities, own and run buses, trams, trains including underground trains, vans, lorries, fire-engines, ambulances, air-craft, ships and hovercraft.

62 Transport
It is one of the Commercial Services or Aids to Trade.

Remember that their initials form the word **WABIT** discussed in Section 1.

63 Advantages of Road Transport
Door-to-door; one loading and one unloading; speedy for short distances; cheaper than rail or air.

64 Advantages of Rail Transport
Inter-City fast and comfortable; freight-liners for fast, regular services; ideal for bulk-carrying; express parcels service, using rail and road; safe and usually punctual.

65 Advantages of Inland Waterways
Ideal for bulky goods and comparatively cheap; quiet; cheaper to maintain routes; can reduce mileage compared with road or rail.

66 Advantages of Sea Transport
Ideal for bulky goods; cheaper than air; can carry more goods and passengers than aircraft.

67 Advantages of Air Transport
Less risk of theft; quickest form of transport for long journeys; ideal for mail and small parcels; less damage to goods.

68 Containerization
Reduces costs of handling, time, labour and damage in respect of goods conveyed over fairly long distances by rail, road, sea and air; very important for international trade, particularly within the Common Market.

69 Terminals
Inter-change facilities and buildings, such as ports for ships, airports for aircraft, termini for trains, etc. Road transport systems require important terminals, too.

70 Rail-Sidings
Used for 'stabling' trains, carriages, wagons, locomotives, etc. Many large firms have factory sidings which connect with British Rail tracks to aid loading and unloading of materials.

71 Choice of Transport
There are eight main points to consider: distance, type of goods, quantity, value of goods, damage or theft risks, cost, urgency, comfort.

Round 1 Questions on Transport

Check your answers by reference to the Term number shown in brackets at the end of each question.

54 The conveyance of passengers, animals and goods from place to place is carried out by .... **(54)**

55 List five types of transport from the list. **(55)**

56 The two divisions of transport are ... and .... **(56)**

57 Inland waterways and sea are two types of transport classification. Name the other three. (57)
58 Transport is owned by three distinct groups. These are ... ...,
... ... and ... . (58)
59 Transport, insurance and banking are three ... ... and transport is one of the five Aids to ... . (62)
60 Name two advantages of using road transport. (63)
61 Name two advantages of using rail transport. (64)
62 List two advantages of using inland waterways for transporting goods. (65)
63 Give two reasons why sea transport is useful. (66)
64 Name two main advantages of air transport. (67)
65 Name two advantages of containerization. (68)
66 Transport terminals are necessary for ... . List four types of transport. (69)
67 Give two reasons for using rail sidings. (70)
68 In choosing the method of transport, there are eight main points to consider. List four of them. (71)

Things to do in your Transport Research and Studies

13 Find out how many British Rail Regions there are. Who owns British Rail and your local public transport?
14 Plan a journey of 200 or more miles by public transport. Write down the times, boarding places, the main towns along your route and the length of time your journey takes. Calculate the fares, stating the single and return charges and any cheap facilities, and add any other interesting details.
15 Using any forms of public and private transport, plan a touring holiday over a period of two weeks and covering about 1,000 miles in Great Britain. Include as many forms of transport as possible as alternative ways of travel and some comparisons of fares.
16 Discuss the ways of transporting goods today and compare them with those used in the past.
17 Draw a map of an area which includes your own town, show all main roads, and mark all train and bus/coach routes and any other transport routes.
18 Find out how goods in local shops and factories are transported in and out of your area.

Round 2 Questions on Transport

Check your answers by reference to the Term number shown in brackets at the end of each question.

19 What kinds of vehicles are used by the business world for the transport of goods? Give a few examples of the goods and the forms of transport generally used to carry them. **(55)**

20 List the eight main points to consider before deciding which of the five types of transport to use for carrying passengers or goods. **(71, 57, 55)**

21 Describe the forms of public transport which are available for people and goods. **(61)**

22 Compare the advantages of using (a) road transport and (b) rail transport for conveying goods. **(63–64)**

23 Now that this country is in the Common Market, can you see any advantages in improving the canal system? **(65, 66, 68)**

24 List as many types of transport you can remember. **(55)**

4

Documents used in Buying and Selling

Documents used in Buying and Selling

72 Letter of Inquiry (or Inquiry, if by telephone)
A request for details of goods required, quantities, prices and terms of payment, which is sent by the buyer to the seller. On page 31 you will find an example of a Letter of Inquiry.

73 Quotation
A reply to the Inquiry, stating goods available, the current prices and delivery dates and terms of payment, which is sent by the seller to the buyer. An example of a Quotation can be found on page 32.

74 Tender
A special kind of Quotation which relates to building or decorating rather than goods.

75 Catalogue
A printed booklet giving details and illustrations of a seller's goods, with or without prices. It is often sent with a Quotation.

76 Price List
A list of prices which may up-date a catalogue to save the cost of reprinting.

77 Order
A form or letter sent by the buyer to the seller which lists the type of goods he wishes to order, the quantities, plus the price of each item. A copy is kept by the buyer. On page 33 you will find an example of an Order.

78 Advice Note
A document sent by the seller to the buyer informing him that the goods have been despatched, the method of transport used and the terms of delivery. The goods are listed but not priced. It is usually posted in advance of the goods.

79 Delivery Note
A document sent by the seller to the buyer with the goods. It gives a list of the goods enclosed, without prices, so that the retailer can check the goods on arrival.

80 Consignment Note

A document supplied by the transporters which is signed by the buyer as a receipt for the goods delivered.

81 Invoice

A bill which is sent by the seller to the buyer, listing the goods purchased on credit, the quantity, the description, the prices, the total cost, the amount of trade discount (may be stated) and the terms of payment. A copy is kept by the seller. (An example of an Invoice is on page 33, see Terms 187 and 188.)

82 Credit Note

An account, usually printed in red, which is sent by the seller to the buyer, which reduces the charge in the invoice because (a) the buyer has been overcharged; (b) goods have been damaged in transit; (c) goods were sent which had not been ordered; or (d) he makes the buyer an allowance for returned packing cases. A copy is kept by the seller. (An example of a Credit Note can be found on page 34.)

83 Debit Note

An account sent by the seller to the buyer which increases the charge in the invoice because he has undercharged the buyer for the goods. A copy is kept by the seller.

84 Statement of Account

An account sent by the seller to the buyer at the end of each month giving details of: any unpaid amount owing from the previous month; the totals of invoices sent to him during the month; any credits for allowances due to the buyer; any debits for undercharges; the amount of cash received from the buyer, and the balance due at the end of the month. A copy is kept by the seller. (You will find an example of a Statement of Account on page 34.)

85 Pro Forma Invoice

It is similar to a quotation but lists the goods as in an ordinary invoice. If the buyer wants to buy the goods, an ordinary invoice can be made out. A pro forma invoice is often sent with goods despatched 'on approval' or on a 'sale or return' basis.

86 Receipt

A form or letter issued by the seller to the buyer when payment is received, showing the date, the sum paid, by whom, and who received the amount.

Round 1 Questions on Documents used in Buying and Selling

Check your answers by reference to the Term number shown in brackets at the end of each question.

69 If a retailer requires details of stock for his shop, he often sends to a seller of goods a ... of .... (**72**)
70 The retailer may telephone the seller for details of the stock he requires—this approach is termed an .... (**72**)
71 The seller's reply to the retailer's letter is often in the form of a .... (**73**)
72 List the four items of information which the seller could give the retailer in his reply. (**73**)
73 A tender is a special kind of .... (**74**)
74 A printed booklet setting out details of a manufacturer's or wholesaler's goods is called a .... (**75**)
75 The printed booklet referred in the previous question may also contain i ... and p .... (**75**)
76 Name two advantages in printing price lists. (**76**)
77 An order form or letter is sent by the ... to the ... listing the types of goods to be purchased. A copy is kept by the .... (**77**)
78 When goods are despatched, the seller usually sends the buyer an ...... to give him advance notice that the goods are on the way. Name three other items of information it may contain. (**78**)
79 When goods arrive the buyer can check them with the enclosed ...... if an invoice does not accompany them. (**79**)
80 The driver of the transport vehicle may ask the buyer for a receipt for the goods he delivers in the form of a .... (**80**)
81 When a seller despatches goods on credit, he sends the buyer a bill (with the goods, or separately by post). This bill is called an .... A copy is kept by the .... (**81**)
82 List seven items which can appear in such a bill. (**81**)
83 If a seller overcharges a buyer, he sends him a .... (**82**)
84 Name three other types of allowances which a seller can give to a buyer which reduce the total of the invoice. (**82**)
85 If a seller undercharges a buyer, he sends the buyer a ...... (**83**)
86 If the buyer is in debt to the seller at the end of any month, the seller will send him a ... of ... . This document contains ... items of information. (**84**)
87 If goods are sent to a buyer 'on approval' or on a 'sale or return' basis, the seller may send him a .... (**85**)
88 A form or letter showing the date, the sum paid, who paid it, and who received it, is called a .... (**86**)

Things to do in your Research and Studies on Documents

19 Study the set of documents illustrated below and the various notes accompanying them.

Bank Paying-in Slip with Counterfoil

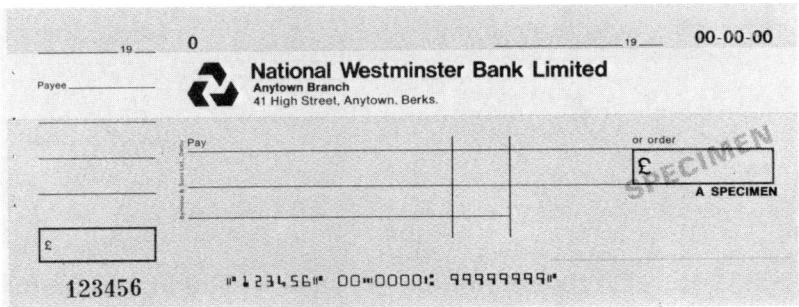

20 Make several copies of the paying-in slip. Fill in the date of the counterfoil (left) and the paying-in slip (right). Write your name, account number and your signature. Fill in the various items you are paying into your current account (both sections, left and right) and total your credit. The bank cashier will check your cash and cheques, etc date-stamp and initial the form, and return the counterfoil to you as a receipt. Re-read Terms 7 and 8 on pages 8 and 9.)

Cheque with counterfoil

21 Make several copies of the cheque then fill in the counterfoil with the date, payee's name, details of payment, and amount of cheque. Next, fill in the cheque itself with the date, payee's name with a line through to the phrase 'or order' to reduce risk of alteration. Write the amount in words, ending with another line drawn after the last word. The amount should be completed in figures (very close together) in the box. (Re-read Terms 6–18 on pages 8–10.)

Bank Statement

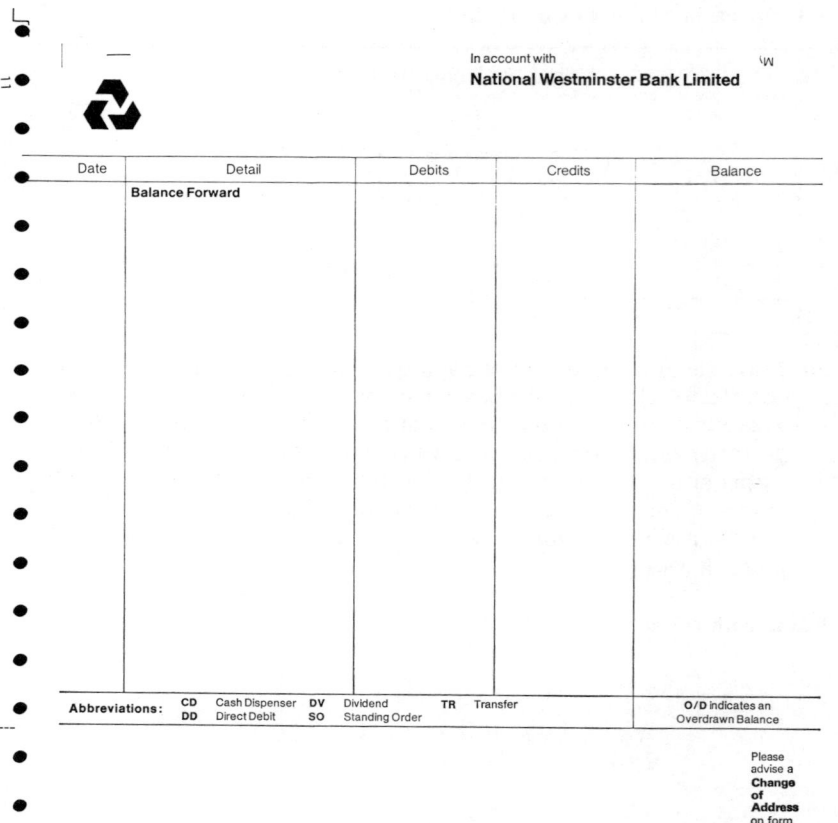

Date	Detail	Debits	Credits	Balance
	Balance Forward			

In account with
National Westminster Bank Limited

Abbreviations: CD Cash Dispenser DV Dividend TR Transfer
DD Direct Debit SO Standing Order

O/D indicates an Overdrawn Balance

Please advise a **Change** of **Address** on form overleaf.

NWB 9903 Revised June 1974

22 Make a copy. In the Receipts (Credits) column write down the total of any paying-in slips you have made out. Record the dates and the balance in hand after each entry (the first balance will be the same as the first receipt). In the Payments (Debits) column write down the total of any cheques you have drawn; record the dates and the balance left over after each entry (under Details, you could write the cheque numbers).

23 Visit a local retailer. Ask him if he could show you some of the documents listed in this section and explain them to you.

24 Study the set of documents illustrated below which are used in buying and selling goods. Draw three columns on a sheet of paper with the headings (a) Document; (b) From; (c) To. Make a list of the documents explained in Terms 72 to 86 and against each of your listed documents fill in columns (b) and (c) with the correct sender and recipient, using the words 'buyer', 'seller' or 'transporter'.

25

Letter of Inquiry

AB RETAILER

Tel **78 55544**   Radio & TV Stockists   66 Station Parade
                                                         EPPING Essex

Our ref AB/234

The Sales Manager   1 January 1978
YZ Wholesalers Ltd
99 Dock Street
TILBURY Essex

Dear Sir

Please send me your catalogue and current price list and state

your terms and delivery dates.

Yours faithfully

(Signed) AB Retailer

Quotation

YZ WHOLESALERS LTD

Tel 037 52 458   99 Dock Street
                                                               TILBURY Essex

Your ref AB/234
Our ref   JM/JC

Messrs AB Retailer   2 January 1978
66 Station Parade
EPPING Essex

Dear Sir

Our catalogue and current price list are enclosed. We can quote

you as follows:

100 GT Radio Sets @ £50 each. If less than 100 ordered, £60 each.

100 GT Record Players @ £80 each. Below 100 ordered, £90 each.

We allow a trade discount of 25% and a cash discount of 5%, and

all deliveries are made within 7 days.

Yours faithfully

YZ WHOLESALERS LTD

(Signed by Sales Manager)

AB RETAILER

Tel **78 55544** Radio & TV Stockists

66 Station Parade
EPPING Essex

ORDER

Our ref AB/Order No 189
Your ref JM/JC 11 January 1978

To The Sales Manager
YZ Wholesalers Ltd
99 Dock Street
Tilbury Essex

Please supply

100 GT Radio Sets @ £50 each.

30 GT Record Players @ £90 each.

Terms are as stated in your Quotation dated 2 January 1978

(Signed) AB Retailer.

YZ WHOLESALERS LTD

Tel 037 52 458

INVOICE No 5

99 Dock Street
TILBURY Essex

Our ref JM/JC/5
Your ref AB/Order 189

To Messrs AB Retailer 18 January 1978
66 Station Parade
Epping Essex

1978				
14 January	100	GT Radio Sets	£50 each	£ 5,000
14 January	30	GT Record Players	£90 each	£ 2,700
				£ 7,700
		Less 25% Trade Discount		£ 1,925
			Total for goods	£ 5,775
			Add 15% VAT	£ 866
Terms: 5% Cash Discount			Total	£ 6,641
one month.				

E. &. O.E.

29

Credit Note (usually printed in red)

YZ WHOLESALERS LTD

Tel 037 52 458
                    CREDIT NOTE No 3   99 Dock Street
                                                    TILBURY Essex

Our ref   JM/JC/5
Your ref   AB/Order 189

To   Messrs AB Retailer   26 January 1978
66 Station Parade
Epping Essex

Allowance for 2 GT Record Players returned due to damage in
transit.   £180
Less 25% Trade Discount   £ 45
                                                               ─────
                                                               £135

                                       Add 15% VAT   £ 20
E. &. O.E.   ─────
                                                               £155
                                                               ═════

30

Statement of Account

YZ WHOLESALERS LTD

Tel 037 52 458
                         STATEMENT   99 Dock Street
                                                    TILBURY Essex
Your ref AB/Order 189
Our ref   JM/JC/5

To Messrs AB Retailer   31 January 1978
66 Station Parade
Epping Essex

1978   Jan 18   Invoice No 5   £6,641
       Jan 26   Credit Note No 3   £   155
                                               ──────
                                               £6,486
                                               ══════
E. &. O.E. Terms: 5%, one month.

31 Write a Letter of Inquiry on behalf of Messrs AB Retailer and ask YZ Wholesalers Ltd for a copy of the current price list with terms and delivery dates. (Study number 25 above.)

32 Prepare a Quotation for YZ Wholesalers Ltd and send it to Messrs AB Retailer. Their terms are now £60 each for any radios ordered and £90 each for any record players ordered with the same discount terms and delivery times as in number 26 above.

33 Make out an Order for Messrs AB Retailer and ask YZ Wholesalers Ltd to supply 20 radio sets. (Study number 27 above.)

34 Prepare an Invoice for YZ Wholesalers Ltd to send to Messrs AB Retailer. (Study number 28 above and make sure that numbers 31, 32, 33 are dated.)

35 Prepare a Credit Note for YZ Wholesalers Ltd to send to Messrs AB Retailer. (Study number 29 above and date the account later than the Invoice date.)

36 Draw up a Statement of Account for YZ Wholesalers Ltd and address it to Messrs AB Retailer. (Study number 30 above and date the Account the last day of the month.)

37 If Messrs AB Retailer pay YZ Wholesalers Ltd within a month of the receipt of the Statement of Account, 5% cash discount can be deducted. Find out how much the retailer would then have to pay the wholesaler and make out a cheque for the amount.

Round 2 Questions on Documents used in Buying and Selling

Check your answers by reference to the Term number shown in brackets at the end of each question.

25 What transactions can take place between a retailer and a wholesaler before goods are ordered? (72–73, 75–76)

26 What information is contained in an Order for goods and who keeps a copy of it? (77)

27 Explain the use of an Advice Note, a Delivery Note and a Consignment Note. (78–80)

28 What are Invoices, Credit Notes and Debit Notes used for and who retains copies of them? (81–83)

29 What information is contained in a Statement of Account and who keeps a copy of it? (84)

30 What is a Pro Forma Invoice and in what circumstances is it used? (85)

31 What information is set out in a formal Receipt? (86)

5

The Services of the Post Office

The Services of the Post Office

87 The Post Office Corporation
It is a business owned by the State and, therefore, it is a Public Enterprise. The services it offers are Direct Services. The Post Office offers services to Industry, Commerce, other Direct Service businesses, and to the Consumer.

88 Post Office Services
Sorts and transports Inland and Overseas post, provides various means of payment, savings and investments, banking through the National Girobank system, telecommunications, and issues licenses for the Government.

89 Postal Services
Inland and overseas letters, parcels, postcards, printed papers, samples, newspapers, registration, recorded delivery, advice (or proof) of delivery, certificate of posting, Post Office boxes, business reply, franking machines, cash on delivery, express services, poste restante (to be called for).

90 Letters and Cards
First and Second Class services (First Class is delivered within one working day, Second Class usually takes at least one day extra for delivery; cheaper rate for Second Class letters posted in bulk).

91 Parcels
Ordinary parcels service and local parcels service (local deliveries being cheaper than those delivered outside the local area).

92 Reduced Postage Rates
Bulk postage; local parcels; there are also special rates for printed papers, samples, and newspapers; literature for the blind is postage free.

93 Registration
The Post Office will pay up to a maximum of £600 compensation for the contents of First Class letters damaged or lost in the post. The registration fees are additional to the postage rate. It

is a form of insurance. Special registered letter envelopes must be used for bank notes, coins, and any documents which can be exchanged for cash.

94 Recorded Delivery

The Recorded Delivery fee of 9p in addition to First and Second Class postage is paid for the service of providing a record of posting and delivering letters and documents. The fee covers compensation up to a £2 maximum provided the lost or damaged contents are not jewellery or money.

95 Advice of Delivery

This is also known as Proof of Delivery. The delivery of any registered letter or Recorded Delivery letter will be reported to the sender on payment of an extra fee for this advice.

96 Certificate of Posting

For a fee of 1p the Post Office will issue a Certificate of Posting for any letter.

97 Post Office Boxes

For a special fee the Post Office will provide an individual or a firm with a numbered box and hold all post in it at the named Post Office instead of delivering it to the addesssee's home or business.

98 Business Reply and Freepost

First and Second Class reply cards and envelopes can be sent to addressees so that they can reply to the senders by post without paying postage. The senders pay the Post Office a special fee plus a little extra charge above the normal postage rate. The cards and envelopes must have two black lines printed on the right-hand side of them with the figure 1 or 2 shown between the lines to indicate First or Second Class postage.

Freepost is similar to Business Reply except that the cost of special stationery is avoided and that all such mail is treated as Second Class. The address of the licensee includes the word 'Freepost' and so no postage need be paid by the addressee.

99 Franking Machines

They are used in place of postage stamps. A licence for their use is issued by the Post Office on payment of a fee. The meter readings are read at a Post Office regularly and the user pays for the postage used. The machines can be hired or purchased.

100 Cash on Delivery

The Post Office will deliver goods to an addressee and take payment for them. The Post Office sends the cash to the sender after charging a service fee.

101 Express Services

Three main services are available: (a) letters and packets handed in at a Post Office for delivery by a special Post Office messenger 'all the way'; (b) letters and packets through the ordinary posting service but delivered by a special Post Office messenger from the addressee's sorting office; (c) letters and packets sent by the first available train involving a special Post Office messenger at either end of the rail journey (called **Railex**).

102 Poste Restante ('To Be Called For')
Letters and packets thus marked can be left regularly at a named Post Office for a three-month period. The addressee must prove his identity when he collects his post.

103 Remittance Services (Means of Payment)
Postage stamps are sometimes used for small payments by post; postal orders up to £10 each (sticking on postage stamps for odd amounts under 5p) are issued uncrossed but can be crossed for sending through the post; Inland Telegraph Money Orders up to £100 each are very safe to send by post (the addressee's Post Office is notified and he cannot obtain payment unless he verifies certain details about the sender); Post Office warrants (similar to cheques); registered post for cash up to £600 (see Term 93, page 36); National Girobank, which is a money transfer service (by using special Girobank forms, one customer's Giro account is debited (charged) with the amount, and another customer is credited (awarded) it).

104 Savings and Investment Services
The Government uses the Post Office to encourage savings in the National Savings Banks (Ordinary Accounts with low interest rate but easy withdrawals; Investment Accounts with high interest rate but one month's withdrawal notice being imposed); Premium Bonds (no interest but chance of winnings by draw— 'Ernie' the electronic computer picks out the winning numbers —and easy withdrawal of savings); National Savings Certificates (full interest rates paid after four or five years' investment); British Savings Bonds (high interest rate with a tax-free bonus after five years' investment); Save-As-You-Earn **(SAYE)** for regular monthly savings for five years with a special bonus payable for seven years' investment. Note that for some savers a lower rate of interest is paid because the savings are protected against inflation—their value is increased in proportion to the rise in prices (measured by the **RPI**—Retail Prices Index).

105 Telecommunications
STD ('*S*ubscriber *T*runk *D*ialling') telephone service; ship telephoning service; mobile radio telephones service; telephone credit card service for subscribers away from home or office; inland and overseas (cables) telegrams service including phototelegrams; Telex (teleprinters are hired out to subscribers) service provides a way of sending written messages quickly over long distances; Datel, by which large amounts of data can be transmitted at great speed from one subscriber to another.

106 Communications

Sending information from one person or business to another. Three forms are (a) written—correspondence, telegrams and cables; (b) spoken—discussion, telephone, radio and television; (c) computer and telecommunication services such as Telex, Datel and satellites (see Term 105 above).

107 Government Business

The Post Office acts as an office for licences, pensions and allowances. For example, retirement pensions are paid out; TV licences are issued.

108 The Post Office Guide

It is the official Post Office information book. The Guide sets out full particulars of all its most important services and the charges for them. You can refer to it for further information about the services described in this Section.

Round 1 Questions on the Services of the Post Office

Check your answers by reference to the number shown in brackets at the end of each question.

89 The Post Office is owned by ... . It is therefore a ... enterprise. **(87)**

90 The services produced by the Post Office are classified as ... services because they are used by industry, commerce, other ... service businesses and the consumer. **(87)**

91 There are ... main Post Office services. Two of these are ... and ... . **(88)**

92 There are ... main postal services; four of these are ... , ... , ... and ... . **(89)**

93 There are two classes of delivery for letters and cards, namely ... and ... . The ... Class mail usually take at least ... day(s) extra for delivery. **(90)**

94 There are two classes of parcels service, namely, ... service and ... service. Which one is the cheaper? ... . **(91)**

95 Reduced postage rates operate for certain classes of mail. Name two of the classes. **(92)**

96 Registration is a form of ... and the Post Office will pay up to £600 ... for First Class mail damaged or lost in the post. Special ... ... envelopes must be used for ... . **(93)**

97 The Post Office will pay up to £2 ... for the loss or damage arising out of posting letters and documents sent by the ... ... service. **(94)**

98 The delivery of mail will be reported to the sender if he pays an extra fee for ... of ... which is also known as ... of .... **(95)**

99 Proof of posting mail can be obtained if the sender hands in an item at a Post Office with a fee of 1p for a ... of .... **(96)**

100 For a special fee an addressee can have his mail placed in a numbered container at a given Post Office. This is called a ... ... **(97)**

101 Two black lines printed on the right-hand side of a card or envelope indicate that the sender has paid a special fee for the ... ... service, which means that he pays the postage on the replies from his customers. As an alternative he may allow his customers to use another reply service called .... **(98)**

102 Busy offices use ... ... in place of postage stamps for outgoing mail. **(99)**

103 The postman will collect the trade charge when delivering goods to an addressee if the sender uses the ... ... service. **(100)**

104 There are ... main express services for letters and packets; the one involving a train is called .... **(101)**

105 The addressee must prove his identity when he collects his mail marked ... ... from a named Post Office. **(102)**

106 There are ... main ways of remitting payments by means of Post Office services. Three of the ways are by ... , ... and .... **(103)**

107 There are ... main ways of saving and investing money through the Post Office. Three of the ways are ... , ... and .... **(104)**

108 There are ... main telecommunications services offered by the Post Office. Three of the services are ... , ... and .... **(105)**

109 What do the letters '**STD**' stand for? **(105)**

110 List the three main forms of communication. **(106)**

111 Name three kinds of Government business which can be transacted in a Post Office. **(107)**

112 A person should refer to the ... ... for full particulars of all the most important services rendered by the Post Office. **(108)**

Things to do in your Post Office Research and Studies

38 Obtain copies of various Post Office forms, or make copies of the forms and fill them in.

39 Make a note of the current First and Second Class postage rates for inland letters and postcards, registration fees, recorded delivery fee, advice of delivery fee, certificate of posting fee, Inland Telegraph Money Order fees and postal order fees.

40 A person wishes to save £10 each month (£120 per annum) for seven years. Make a rough calculation of the amount of interest

he can earn in seven years on each form of investment available through the Post Office.

41 Look at a Post Office Guide. Make up your own notebook on the various Post Office services, forms, instructions and rules.

Round 2 Questions on the Services of the Post Office

Check your answers by reference to the Term number shown in brackets at the end of each question.

32 List some of the main services which the Post Office provides for business. **(88)**

33 What type of enterprise is the Post Office and who owns it? **(87)**

34 Describe the main differences between the Post Office registration service and its recorded delivery service. **(93–95)**

35 What advantages are there to the sender of post and the addressee if the Business Reply or Freepost service of the Post Office is used? Describe the two services **(98)**

36 What is the main difference between the Post Office box service and the poste restante service? **(97, 102)**

37 Name the advantages to the trader and to the customer if the Post Office **COD** Service is used. **(100)**

38 Explain the Post Office service called 'Railex'. **(101)**

39 Explain how you would send £60 in £5 notes by letter post and state why the Inland Telegraph Money Order is a safe way of remitting such an amount by post if the sender does not wish to send the addressee a cheque. **(93, 103)**

40 Explain why Premium Savings Bonds differ from the other forms of National Savings. **(104)**

41 Telex is one of the main Post Office telecommunications services. Briefly explain how the system operates. **(105)**

42 Describe the main three forms of communications. **(106)**

43 (a) What form of savings service is provided by the Post Office with easy withdrawal facilities but only a low rate of interest paid on deposits and (b) what type of savings service is available for regular monthly savings with high interest rate? Compare the advantages of both forms of savings in the Post Office. **(104)**

44 Why is the Post Office Guide such a useful book? Give details of some of the information contained in it. **(108)**

6

Advertising

Advertising Terms

Term

109 Advertising

Advertising is one of the Commercial Services or Aids to Trade. This stands for *W*arehousing, *A*dvertising, *B*anking, *I*nsurance and *T*ransport (**WABIT**).

110 Purpose of Advertising

To assist industry, commerce, and direct services in the buying and selling of goods and services; also it helps the consumer in the buying of goods and services.

111 Advantages of Advertising

It gives information about goods and services which are available; it persuades people to buy; it introduces new products; it assists mass production, which should mean cheaper goods for the buyer and increased profits for the seller.

112 Some Disadvantages of Advertising

It encourages 'impulse' buying. It makes some consumers dissatisfied with their status. It encourages the purchase of harmful products and can increase the price of some goods.

113 Motives to which Advertisers Appeal

Romance, hero worship, ambition, success, easy living, social acceptance.

114 Ways of Advertising

Window displays, delivery vans advertisements, loss leaders, newspaper advertisements including classified advertisements, magazine advertisements, periodical sales, catalogues, cinema advertisements, wrapping-paper and bags, circulars and bills, canvassers, calendars, illuminations, free gifts and bargains, transport advertisements on vehicles and stations, sandwichmen, demonstrations, hoarding posters, radio advertisements, television advertisements, branded goods (trade marks), direct mail.

115 Mass Media Advertising

Television, commercial radio and newspapers are three methods of large-scale advertising intended to reach the maximum number of people.

116 Advertising Association and The Institute of Public Relations

These organizations draw up and publish codes of advertising practice to protect the consumer. Their members and other organizations join together to administer the British Code of Advertising Practice. The Code is a set of rules to ensure that advertising is legal, clean, honest and truthful.

117 Mass Production

Using modern machinery, using one man for one job for each line along the production belt, and producing very large quantities of goods at reduced costs. Advertising enables manufacturers to find markets for mass-produced goods.

118 Impulse Buying

Buying on the spur of the moment without considering all of the facts.

Round 1 Questions on Advertising

Check your answers by reference to the Term number shown in brackets at the end of each question.

113 Advertising is one of the Commercial Services or Aids to Trade. How many services are there? **(109)**

114 The purpose of advertising is to assist industry, ... and ... ... in the buying and selling of goods and services and it also helps the ... . **(110)**

115 There are ... main advantages of advertising goods and services. **(111)**

116 Advertising encourages ... buying; it also encourages the purchase of ... . **(112)**

117 Romance, hero worship and easy living are three motives to which advertisers appeal. Name the other three. **(113)**

118 Write down five ways of advertising goods for sale. **(114)**

119 Advertising intended to reach the maximum number of people is called ... ... advertising. **(115)**

120 The Advertising Association and The Institute of Public Relations draw up and publish ... of advertising ... to protect the..... The ... is a set of ... to help advertising to be ..., ... , honest and ... . **(116)**

121 Producing goods in very large quantities with the aid of modern machinery and specialization of labour is called ... . **(117)**

122 If a person buys goods on the spur of the moment, his act is called ... . **(118)**

Things to do in your Advertising Research and Studies

42 Collect some cuttings of advertisements and trade marks from circulars, newspapers and magazines. Find out if any of them influence your friends and relations when they decide to buy goods.

43 Inquire at a newspaper office about details of the cost of various advertisements.

44 Refer to the list of methods of advertising. Make a report on those used in your own locality.

45 Which television advertisements appeal to you, your friends and your relations? Prepare a chart listing the most popular product advertisements.

46 Find out which ways of advertising are used by one or two of your local retailers.

47 Find six cuttings of advertisements to cover the list of six motives to which advertisers appeal.

Round 2 Questions on Advertising

Check your answers by reference to the Term number shown in brackets at the end of each question.

45 What is the purpose of advertising and what advantages are gained by those who buy and sell goods and services? (110–111)

46 List the motives to which advertisers appeal and describe some of the disadvantages of advertising. (112–113)

47 What types of businesses spend money on mass media advertising and what advantages do they gain from it? (110–111, 115, 117)

48 Why is it essential to have a code of advertising practice? (112–113, 116)

49 If you intended to start a local business, what ways of advertising would you use? Give reasons for your choice. (114–15)

50 As a consumer what advantages do you derive from advertisements? (110–111)

51 Why are branded goods a good form of advertising? (111, 114) Describe some branded goods which interest you. (115)

52 Is the public very much influenced by advertisements? Do they believe in all the advertisements they see or hear about? Express some of your own feelings about advertisements. (111–113, 115, 118)

7

Warehousing and Storage

Warehousing and Storage Terms

Term

119 Warehousing and Storage
Warehousing is <u>one</u> of the Commercial Services or Aids to Trade. *W*arehousing; *A*dvertising; *B*anking; *I*nsurance; *T*ransport **(WABIT).**

120 Purpose of Warehouses
They are used for the storage of goods on a large scale. The producers and manufacturers of goods can disperse their goods to wholesalers' warehouses to make room for new products.

121 Who owns Warehouses
Producers and manufacturers for storage of goods and spare parts; wholesalers for storage of a great variety of goods each in large quantities (in bulk); discount stores for storing bulk supplies which they sell direct to consumers at discount prices; mail order firms who sell their goods direct to the consumer by means of catalogues and cash-on-delivery services; retailers for the storage of goods to replenish the stock for sale in their shops.

122 Advantages of Warehouses
They can be spread around the country as storage centres; retailers can visit wholesalers' warehouses and select produce and goods from a variety of producers and manufacturers; retailers usually have little storage space, therefore they can make regular visits to large warehouses—small retailers can obtain good cash discounts by purchasing on a cash-and-carry basis (see Section 9, Retailing, page 54).

123 Bonded Warehouses
Usually placed in large ports to store dutiable goods. These are goods on which customs duty must be paid before they leave the warehouse. The owner of the goods signs a bond (promise) not to sell them before duty is paid. While in the warehouse the goods are protected by the Customs Officers.

124 Advantages of Bonded Warehouses

Dutiable imports need not delay a ship's unloading of its cargo of goods—they can be placed in the warehouse under the supervision of the Customs Officers. Such goods as wines can be bottled and packed and then inspected by possible buyers before duty is paid on them; also tobacco can be made into saleable goods before duty is paid on it. Duty is not paid on these goods until the importer sells them and recovers the duty from the consumer.

Round 1 Questions on Warehousing and Storage

Check your answers by reference to the Term number shown in brackets at the end of each question.

123 Warehousing is one of the ...... or Aids to .... How many of these are there? (119)

124 Warehouses are used for the ... of ... on a ... scale. The producers and manufacturers of goods can ... their goods to ... warehouses to make room for new .... (120)

125 Producers and manufacturers own warehouses; also wholesalers own warehouses for storing a great variety of goods each in ... quantities (called ...). Other owners of warehouses are ... stores, ... order firms and retailers. (121)

126 Retailers can visit wholesalers' warehouses and obtain cash ... by purchasing goods on a ...-and-... basis. (122)

127 Dutiable goods can be placed in a warehouse in a port under the supervision of the Customs Officers. Such a warehouse is known as a .... (123–124)

128 Wines and tobacco can be prepared for sale during the time they are in a ... warehouse. The Customs ... is not paid on them until the ... sells them. (124)

Things to do in your Warehousing and Storage Research and Studies

48 Visit a wholesale warehouse to see how goods are stored and sold.

49 Visit several local retail shops to inquire if the owners visit wholesale warehouses to select some of their goods. Discuss the cash-and-carry system with them.

50 Contact shipping companies, importers, large wine merchants, tobacco companies, etc with a view to obtaining information about bonded warehouses. Arrange to visit a bonded warehouse.

Round 2 Questions on Warehousing and Storage

Check your answers by reference to the Term number shown in brackets at the end of each question.

53 Give two reasons for having warehouses and list the kinds of businesses which own them. (120–121)

54 Write about the advantages of warehouses to producers, manufacturers and retailers. (120–122)

55 Give reasons for the existence of bonded warehouses and the uses to which they are put. (123–124)

8

Production

Production Terms

Term

125 Production

Production is the creation of goods or services to satisfy people's wants.

126 Producers

Producers are those who work for profit or a wage or salary by producing goods or services. They are known as employers if they own a business and employees if they earn a wage or salary. The Chairman of the Coal Board, the coal-miner and the clerical staff at the Coal Board are producers in an extractive industry. A tool-maker and a manager in the motor industry are producers in a manufacturing industry. Workers in Warehouses, Advertising, Banking, Insurance, and Transport (**WABIT**) are producers in Commercial Services. Doctors, dentists and teachers are examples of people in a Direct Service occupation.

127 Classification of Occupations

All work carried out by owners of businesses or employees can be divided into three branches of production: (a) Industry; (b) Commerce; (c) Direct Services.

128 Industry

All work producing minerals and oil from the land and the sea, and timber and pulp from the forests is classified as extractive industry. Manufacturing, assembling and processing goods are classified as manufacturing industry. Laundering and catering are services classified as service industry.

129 Commerce

All activities producing trade (buying and selling) and commercial services (Aids to Trade) are classified as Commerce.

130 Trade

All activities relating to buying and selling goods. Trade is divided into (a) Home Trade (Wholesale and Retail) and (b) Overseas Trade (Import and Export).

131 Commercial Services (Aids to Trade)
Home and international trade depends very much on the help of the commercial services: *W*arehousing and Storage; *A*dvertising; *B*anking; *I*nsurance; *T*ransport (**WABIT**). (Re-read the Sections on these services.)

132 Direct Services
Employers and employees in these services provide them for industry, commerce, other direct services, and the consumer. They include dustmen, dentists, doctors, teachers, nurses, local authority workers, lawyers and Members of Parliament.

133 Chain of Production
People are dependent upon each other for goods and services. They are producers and consumers at the same time and, in effect, form links in a chain which starts with the extractive industry (say, the farmer), and ends with the home trade (say, the local retail shop) and ourselves as buyers (consumers). The links in between are manufacturers, wholesalers, warehousemen, insurers, bankers, advertisers, transporters, and the direct services (doctors, dustmen, teachers, etc).

Round 1 Questions on Production

Check your answers by reference to the Term number shown in brackets at the end of each question.

129 Production means producing ... or ... to satisfy ... . **(125)**

130 People who work for profit or a wage or salary are producers of ... or ... . They are known as ... if they own a business and ... if they earn a wage or salary. **(126)**

131 The Chairman of the Coal Board, the coal-miner and the clerical staff at the Coal Board are classified as ... in an ... industry. **(126)**

132 Workers in Warehouses, Advertising, Banking, Insurance and Transport are ... in services classified as ... . **(126)**

133 The three branches of production are ..., ... and Direct Services. **(127)**

134 All work producing food from the land and the sea is classified as ... . Assembling and processing goods are classified as ... . Laundering and catering are services classified as ... . **(128)**

135 All work producing trade and aids to trade is classified as ... . **(129)**

136 The four branches of trade are ..., ..., ... and ... . **(130)**

137 The commercial services (aids to trade) are ..., ..., ..., ... and ... . Name the five. **(131)**

138 Dustmen, dentists, doctors and others produce services classified as ... . **(132)**

139 People are producers and consumers at the same time and in effect form links in the ... of ... . These links start with the ... industry and end with the ... trade and ourselves as ... . **(133)**

140 List ten links in the chain of production, including the farmer, retail shop and the consumer. **(133)**

Things to do in your Research and Studies in Production

51 Compile a list of thirty or more producers of goods or services (examples: farmers, caterers, dustmen). Head three columns as set out below:

Industry   Commerce   Direct Services

and place your producers in their correct columns. Head your work:

Production

52 Write down the heading:

Commercial Services (Aids to Trade)

Then head five columns as under:

Warehousing   Advertising   Banking
Insurance   Transport

Make a list of your local businesses which are classified as Commercial Services. You will therefore not include shops (trade), factories (industry), dentists, local council workers, etc (Direct Services). Place the producers under the proper headings.

53 Make a list of your local Direct Services. You will include education (schools and colleges), recreation (parks and sports fields), dentists, etc.

Round 2 Questions on Production

Check your answers by reference to the Term number shown in brackets at the end of each question.

56 Give a brief definition of the term Production. **(125–126)**

57 Who are the producers of goods and services? Give some examples. **(126–132)**

58 Production can be divided into three main branches. Write down the three headings and place the following list of producers in their correct groups:

farmer; train driver; dentist; car worker; teacher; miner; banker; Coal Board typist; typist in a department store; typist in a hospital; wholesaler; retailer. **(126–132)**

59 Industry produces goods and services which are classified under three headings. Write down those headings and give two examples of production in each column. **(128)**

60 Make a list of all the main divisions and subdivisions of Commerce. **(129–131)**

61 Direct Services is one of the three sections of Production. List some of the producers who are classified under the heading of Direct Services (give at least five examples). **(132)**

62 What do you understand from the term 'Chain of Production'? **(133)**

9

Home Trade

Home Trade Terms

Term

134 Types of Retailer

Small shops (unit shops); department stores; multiple or chain stores; co-operative retail society shops; self-service stores, supermarkets and hypermarkets; local retail markets (stalls); mail order houses; discount stores; mobile shops; hawkers and pedlars; door-to-door salesmen; manufacturers' retail shops; vending machines.

135 Small Shops

They account for about half of all the retail business in this country. Friendly relationship with consumers; personal service; often near consumers' homes (saves time and fares); extended shopping hours; cut-prices by joining wholesalers' voluntary chains (such as Spar, VG and Mace)—cash-and-carry wholesale warehouses cut down paper work and retailer obtains a good cash discount. Unit shops may have a delivery service, may allow credit arrangements on the spot and carry out local repairs to goods. Some disadvantages are: prices of goods may be much higher; range of goods usually less than larger shops; lack of capital may prevent expansion; competition often forces close-down or take-over by larger shops. Small shops are usually owned by one person called a sole trader. (You will find further explanation in Section 13, page 74).

136 Department Stores

This type of retail outlet can be likened to several shops under one roof owned by one business unit, usually a limited company. (Look ahead to Section 13, page 74, for further information.) Examples are Selfridges and Harrods. Department Stores buy in bulk and sell a wide range of goods and services. Some advantages: regular delivery services by some stores and orders can be 'phoned through'; customers can open credit accounts and also use cheque cards; shoppers are free to walk around the store and have refreshments there; expert buyers and sellers are employed. Banking facilities and travel and theatre bookings are often available. Some disadvantages: high rents for premises and luxury facilities increase the overheads; store must be in a busy street and near public transport and car parking; may be lack of personal service and sometimes an unfriendly atmosphere; numerous staff engaged on non-selling work, such as clerical, secretarial, accounting, debt-collecting, detective work.

137 Multiple or Chain Stores

These shops have been 'multiplied' to form a chain—some chains have over two thousand shops (the shop front itself is a nation-wide advertisement). Examples are Boots the Chemists, W H Smith & Sons, Woolworth, MacFisheries. Two types of Chain Stores: variety chain stores such as Woolworth and British Home Stores; specialist chain stores such as Sainsbury's, Boots the Chemists and MacFisheries. A Multiple Store is owned by one business unit (usually a limited company—see Section 13, Business Units, page 74) and has a separate Head Office and branch managers report to it. Some advantages: bulk buying and/or manufacturing of their own goods means lower costs of goods and so lower prices can be charged to consumers; companies selling their own manufactured goods use their own labels—branded goods advertise themselves; staff can be moved around and bad trade in a particular area can be offset by a high sales turnover in another. Some disadvantages: branch manager and his staff are controlled by a remote Head Office; credit terms not often available to consumers; the atmosphere is often less friendly than that at the small shop; many of the disadvantages of departmental stores also apply to multiple stores.

138 Co-operative Retail Societies

These Societies are owned and run by members who are also customers. Each member has a share number and a share account into which he must pay a minimum amount of money; each member has only one vote and they appoint a Management Committee which is accountable to them at meetings held during each year. The net profits (called 'surplus') are used to provide educational, social and welfare facilities for members and the public, to support political activities through the Co-operative Party and the Labour Party, and to provide members with dividend stamps which can be cashed, exchanged for goods, or credited to the members' share accounts. Some advantages of Co-operative Societies: consumers own and run them; dividend stamps are common to all the Societies in the country; many products are from tea plantations, farms, dairies and factories owned by the Co-operative Societies (some are owned by Production Societies or Wholesale Societies); Co-op products are sold all over the country; shops are often near homes and deliveries of some foods are made. Some disadvantages: most members do not vote, so a society may be controlled by people with strong political views without being efficient in running businesses; less than half of the goods sold are from non-Co-operative businesses, but even so the Societies are still acting as retailers for their competitors (examples: CWS biscuits are sold alongside Crawfords'; CWS butter is sold alongside Anchor butter)—such reluctance to purchase Co-operative Wholesale Society (CWS) goods prevents the Society from producing more goods on a massive scale which could mean much lower prices.

139 Self-Service Stores and Supermarkets

These retailers encourage 'impulse' buying through attractive display. Bulk buying means that prices are often lower than in smaller shops. Self-service is 'do-it-yourself' shopping and customers are free to walk around without any obligation to purchase goods. Small shops, chain stores, co-operative retail societies and department stores are often partly or wholly self-service nowadays. A Supermarket requires a large capital to maintain the business, so it is usually owned by a limited liability company (examples: Tesco and Sainsbury's—see Section 13, Business Units, page 74). Advantages of Supermarkets to retailer: can buy in bulk at much reduced prices; can produce own products and pack own brands. Advantages of Super-markets to consumers: self-service is quick at most times; goods are on view with prices marked; reduced prices in the form of discounts or special packing. Some disadvantages to consumers: the personal touch between the owner or staff and the customer is often lacking; credit is seldom given; delivery service to customers' home seldom available; single people with low incomes find difficulty in purchasing very small quantities and elderly people often need the help of a shop-assistant. Hyper-markets are large supermarkets. They have 50,000 or more square feet of floor-space and sell a wider range of goods on a department store scale. Hypermarkets are often in an area which is easily accessible to motor vehicles and has room for plenty of parking to enable cash-and-carry business to be transacted.

140 Local Retail Markets

There are many ancient rights and laws in various parts of our country relating to street trading. Market days attract customers and stall-owners, and yearly fairs also attract large crowds. Stall-owners and hirers do not have to pay heavy rents, heating and lighting bills, so they are able to offer bargains to consumers, especially if there is competition between two or more nearby stall-owners.

141 Mail Order Houses

There is no personal contact between the seller and the buyer, but the seller may have agents who have mail order catalogues to lend to interested customers. The three ways of purchasing goods are (a) through the local agent who may also collect the selling price in one payment or by instalments, (b) cash with order, with 'guarantee of satisfaction or money back' protection, and (c) cash on delivery (**COD**) when payment is made to the postman (see Post Office Services, Section 5, page 36). Advantages to customers: a good service for people living in remote areas; customers can select goods from illustrated catalogues at leisure and some become agents and earn commission on sales; some products are not normally stocked by the average retailer; credit is provided for those who cannot afford cash down. Disadvantages: no personal contact between the seller and the customer; advertising and printing costs are high; customers are not always sure of the quality or the look of the goods illustrated or advertised. Advantages to seller: expensive shops are not required; newspaper and magazine readers provide a very wide market; bulk orders to manufacturers mean cheaper purchases; no delivery vans required as goods are transported by the Post Office, British Rail, National Carriers Ltd or other road transporters. Disadvantages to seller: costs of producing catalogues and advertising in newspapers are very high; large stocks may cause heavy financial losses if goods are not sold because they go out of fashion or because prices fall.

142 Discount Houses (also known as Discount Stores)

These are large warehouse-type stores which started in this country round about 1960 and are now very popular. Overheads (expenses) are cut to a minimum to enable goods to be sold at very much reduced prices. Ideal method of buying for car-owners as they are mostly cash-and-carry businesses. Discount Houses are popular for hi-fi equipment, household equipment such as refrigerators, and various other types of household goods. Some disadvantages are: credit facilities and delivery service are not always available and often there is little after-sales service.

143 Mobile Shops

Bakers and dairymen are two examples, but in country areas retailers and farmers convey other goods direct to consumers' homes. Where homes are not close to shops and when customer is tied to home by age, sickness or young children this can be very useful. Mobile shops are usually understood to be hawkers with vehicles, but pedlars with cases containing goods should be included under this heading. A mobile trader often works outside the normal shop hours, which benefits people out at work all day, but he carries a limited amount and choice of goods.

144 Vending Machines

Automatic machines are found on railway stations, in factories, outside shops and in many other places. Machine vending is another form of self-service and machines can be used for the sale of many types of goods in addition to chocolate, milk, hot and cold drinks and books. Some advantages: shopkeepers' sales are increased after closing times; consumers find them useful at work, before going on a journey by public transport, or after shop-hours. Some disadvantages: heavy capital costs of machines and their maintenance often result in goods costing the consumer more than the prices in the shops; misuse or vandalism can make them unprofitable.

145 Home Trade Divisions

There are two divisions: (a) retail trade (see Term 134, page 54), (b) wholesale trade (see Terms below). (See Term 130, page 50.)

146 Wholesaler

Wholesalers are middlemen, buying goods from the primary producers and the manufacturers in bulk and selling them to retailers and sometimes the consumer in smaller quantities.

147 Some Advantages of Wholesalers

Primary producers, such as farmers and fishermen, and manufacturers can disperse their goods to wholesalers' warehouses and markets all over the country to make room for new products; retailers can travel to local warehouses to inspect and select goods from a variety of producers; retailers can purchase goods from wholesalers on a much reduced cash-and-carry basis; retailers can buy goods on credit from wholesalers and seek advice on the market situation on a range of items; wholesalers can supply manufacturers and primary producers with information about the demand for various goods at different seasons of the year. Some wholesalers package goods, such as tea and coffee, ready for sale by retailers. Wholesalers can pay producers and manufacturers for bulk goods delivered immediately (they then earn a cash discount) which places ready cash in the producers' hands in exchange for large stocks of goods. (See also Term 135, page 54.)

148 Wholesale Markets

These are special places, mostly in towns, where producers, wholesalers and retailers can meet to buy and sell specific commodities. Examples: fruit and vegetable wholesale markets; fish wholesale markets (Billingsgate is one); meat wholesale markets (Smithfield is one). Wholesale commodities are not normally sold to consumers at wholesale markets—do not become confused with local retail markets where retailers sell their goods from stalls to the consumers. (See Terms 130 and 140, pages 50 and 56.)

149 Wholesale Warehouses

They are spread out all over the country to serve retailers in their areas. Many are sited near main roads or alongside railways and some wholesalers operate fleets of vans to collect goods from producers and to deliver them to their retailers. (See also Terms 120–122, page 46, Term 142, page 57, and Term 135, page 54, for further information.)

Round 1 Questions on Home Trade

Check your answers by reference to the Term number shown in brackets at the end of each question.

141 There are ... main types of retailer. **(134)**

142 There are several advantages and disadvantages in having small retail shops (called 'unit shops'). List three advantages and three disadvantages. **(135)**

143 A Department Store is a type of ... outlet made up of several shops under one roof owned by one ... unit (usually a ... company). Examples are ... and ... . **(136)**

144 List three advantages and three disadvantages of Department Stores. **(136)**

145 Multiple or Chain Stores have been '...' to form a ... . Examples are ... and ... . Two types of Chain Stores: ... Chain Stores such as ... and ... ; ... Chain Stores such as ... and ... . A Multiple Store is owned by one ... ... (usually a limited ...) . **(137)**

146 Give two advantages and two disadvantages in having Multiple Stores or Shops. **(137)**

147 Co-operative Retail Societies are owned and run by their ... who are also ... . Each ... has a ... number and a ... account and each ... has a vote and appoints a ... . **(138)**

148 The net profits of a Co-operative Retail Society are called a ... and after setting aside certain funds it provides members with ... ... which can be ... , exchanged for ..., or ... to the members' ... . **(138)**

149 List two advantages and two disadvantages in having Co-operative Societies. **(138)**

150 Self-service is '...-...-...' shopping. **(139)**

151 A Supermarket requires a large ... to maintain the business, so it is usually owned by a limited ... . **(139)**

152 Write down two advantages and two disadvantages of Super-markets. **(139)**

153 Hypermarkets are large .... They have 50,000 or more square feet of ... . They are often in an area which is easily accessible to motor vehicles with plenty of parking to enable ...-...- carry business to be transacted. **(139)**

154 Stall-owners and hirers do not have to pay heavy overheads, so they are able to offer ... to .... **(140)**

155 List the three ways of purchasing goods from a Mail Order House. **(141)**

156 State three advantages and three disadvantages in having Mail Order Houses. **(141)**

157 Discount Stores (Discount Houses) are large ...-... stores. Overheads (...) are cut right down to enable goods to be sold at very much ... . **(142)**

158 Name one type of goods sold at Discount Stores and mention two disadvantages in using them. **(142)**

159 Give two examples of Mobile Shops and mention one advantage and one disadvantage of them. **(143)**

160 Write down two advantages and two disadvantages of automatic vending machines. **(144)**

161 Name the two divisions of home trade. **(145)**

162 Wholesalers are ..., buying goods from the ... producers and the ... in bulk and selling them to ... and sometimes the ... in smaller quantities. **(146)**

163 Make a list of four advantages in having the services of whole-salers. **(147)**

164 The special places where wholesalers and retailers can meet to buy and sell specific commodities are known as ... . **(148)**

165 Wholesale Warehouses are spread out all over the country to serve .... Some wholesalers operate ... of ... to collect goods from ... and to deliver them to .... **(149)**

Things to do in your Research and Studies in Home Trade

54 Study the list of the main types of retailer. Make headings, one for each type of retailer, and write down under the correct heading as many businesses as possible. To start you off here are a few examples: Littlewoods (Mail Order House), EMI (Manufacturer's Retail Shop), Tesco's (Supermarket) and Marks & Spencer (Multiple Store).

55 Discuss why certain small shops still exist in your neighbour-hood and are not driven out of business by the larger types of retailer.

56 Compare the prices in your local Co-operative shop with those in nearby shops and discuss why some people prefer to trade with the Society and why others prefer to trade with their competitors.

57 Discuss the reasons why so many customers use the local supermarket.

Round 2 Questions on Home Trade

Check your answers by reference to the Term number shown in brackets at the end of each question.

63 Make a list of the main types of retailer and write a few lines about any two of them. (**134–144**)

64 Compare department stores with multiple stores. (**136–137**)

65 Explain why co-operative societies differ from the other types of retailers in terms of ownerships and control. (**138**)

66 Compare the self-service at supermarkets with the personal service available at some unit shops and explain why both forms of retailing can exist. (**135, 139**)

67 Describe a local retail market and try to account for the attractiveness of this type of retailing. (**140**)

68 Why do many consumers use mail order houses? (**141**)

69 If you wished to purchase a record-player, what arguments should be put forward before you decided to carry out the transaction at a discount store (discount house)? (**142**)

70 Are mobile shops really necessary nowadays? Could consumers in all parts of the country obtain all their goods from the customary shops? Give your own views on mobile shops. (**143**)

71 Is it worthwhile maintaining and supplying automatic vending machines? Where are the best sites for them? Give your own views on vending machines. (**144**)

72 Why are wholesalers called 'middlemen' and why are they useful? Why are there wholesale markets and wholesale warehouses? (**146–149**)

10

Overseas Trade—Imports and Exports

Overseas Trade—Import and Export Terms

Term

150 Commodity Markets (also called Commodity Exchanges)

These Markets or Exchanges are mostly in the City of London, but others are in great ports such as Liverpool. They hold daily sales of raw materials, such as corn (Corn Exchange), tea, coffee, cocoa, sugar, wool, cotton, spices, tobacco, ivory, rum, copper, lead, zinc, tin. Other metals all have Exchanges or Markets. No goods go into these Markets—in fact, some never come into Great Britain. They are bought and sold either by samples or description. Auction sales are common.

151 Baltic Exchange

This is a market for buying and selling shipping and air space for imports and exports. It is also known as a Freight Market—the word 'freight' meaning cargo or the charge for transporting goods. The Baltic Exchange also contains an Oil and Oilseeds Market. Shipowners and airline-owners, or their agents, meet at the Exchange the owners of goods to be exported or imported (or the agents of the owners) to fix transport costs.

152 Factors and Agents

These people are middlemen (see also Term 146, page 58). Merchants are middlemen but, like wholesalers, they own the goods they handle. Factors and Agents are also called Mercantile Agents. The difference between them is that a Factor handles goods he is selling on behalf of the owners, whereas an Agent arranges the sale of goods on behalf of the owners without handling the goods.

153 EEC (European Economic Community)

This Group is commonly known as the Common Market. West Germany, France, Italy, Belgium, Holland, Luxemburg, Denmark, Ireland, and Great Britain (nine countries) signed the Treaty of Rome, under which imports and exports within their countries must be duty-free and they must apply a **CET** (see Term 154 below).

154 CET (Common External Tariff)

This is a duty on imports from all non-EEC countries. Our country does have at present some special trading arrangements with some of our Commonwealth countries. It should be noted that not all Western European countries are in the EEC but that Spain, Portugal and Greece may join it in due course.

155 Balance of Trade

This term is used to indicate the difference between what we pay for the import of goods and what we receive for the export of goods. Such imports and exports of goods are called visible imports and visible exports. If our visible imports are higher than our visible exports, our country has an adverse Balance of Trade; if our visible exports are higher than our visible imports, then we have a favourable Balance of Trade (which means that we are not in debt to the outside world).

156 Balance of Payments

This term is used to indicate how much we owe the outside world or how much they owe us after we have added to, or taken away from, the Balance of Trade the difference between our invisible exports and invisible imports. We sell abroad services (shipping, insurance, technical advice, tourist trade, etc) which are called invisible exports because you cannot see them as you can goods—these services are exports though because we receive income from them. We also buy services from abroad (American technical advice is one example) which are called invisible imports—these services are called imports because we have to pay for them in the same way as we have to pay for visible imports (goods). The Balance of Payments figure is therefore the difference between our total exports and our total imports, which can be a favourable figure or an unfavourable (adverse) figure. Examples:

*=millions

	(I)	
Total	Exports	£500m*
	Imports	400m
	Balance of payments	100m (Favourable)

	(II)	
Total	Imports	£550m
	Exports	400m
	Balance of Payments	150m

(Unfavourable or Adverse)

Sometimes, this country has an adverse Balance of Trade, but its favourable invisible exports converts the unfavourable figure into a favourable Balance of Payments figure. It is important to understand that the countries of the world are dependent upon each other for goods and services and that in the main they must try to match their import figures with their export figures to avoid seeking loans or finding other ways of settling their debts with each other.

Round 1 Questions on Overseas Trade

Check your answers by reference to the Term number shown in brackets at the end of each question.

166 Commodity Markets (also called Commodity Exchanges) sell and buy large quantities of goods by ... or description. There are Commodity Exchanges for ... and ... (give two examples). **(150)**

167 The Market for buying and selling shipping and air space for imports and exports is known as the ... Exchange. It is also called a ... Market. This Exchange also contains an ... and ... Market. **(151)**

168 Factors and Agents are ... . Merchants are ... but like wholesalers they ... the goods they handle. Factors and Agents are also called ... . A Factor ... goods, whereas an Agent arranges the sale of goods without ... them. **(152)**

169 The letters EEC form the abbreviation for the ... ... This Group is commonly known as ... ... **(153)**

170 List the present nine countries which belong to the EEC. **(153)**

171 The letters CET form the abbreviation for the ... ... and is a ... on ... from all non-EEC countries. **(154)**

172 The difference between what a country pays for imports of goods and what it receives for the export of goods is termed ... of ... . **(155)**

173 Goods imported are called ... imports; goods exported are called ... exports. **(155)**

174 If the cost of imported goods is higher than the amount we receive for exported goods, our country has an ... ... of ... . If it is the other way round, our country has a ... ... of ... . **(155)**

175 We sell abroad services such as shipping, insurance, technical advice and tourist trade. These services are called ... exports. If we buy services from abroad such as American technical advice, these services are called ... imports. **(156)**

176 The Balance of Payments figure is the difference between our

total ... and our total ... , which can be a ... figure or
an ... (...) figure. (**156**)

177 Sometimes, this country has an ... Balance of Trade, but its
favourable ... exports converts the unfavourable balance into
a favourable ... of ... . (**156**)

Things to do in your Research and Studies in Overseas Trade

58 Make a list of the main Commodity Markets (Exchanges).

59 Draw a rough map of Europe and colour in the countries which
belong to the European Economic Community (EEC = The
Common Market).

60 Copy and fill in the answers in the following statements:

Visible Exports	£350m
Visible Imports	300m
Balance of Trade	(State whether it is favourable or adverse)
Invisible Exports	£150m
Invisible Imports	100m
Difference	
Balance of Trade, as above	
Balance of Payments	(State whether it is favourable or adverse)

(Check your answer with Example I in Term 156, page 63.)

61 Copy and fill in the answers and make similar statements as
those in number 60 above:

Visible Imports	£500m
Visible Exports	300m
Balance of Trade	(State whether it is favourable or adverse)
Invisible Exports	£100m
Invisible Imports	50m
Difference	(State whether it is favourable or adverse)
Balance of Trade, as above	
Balance of Payments	(State whether it is favourable or adverse)

(Check your answer with Example II in Term 156, page 63.)

Round 2 Questions on Overseas Trade

Check your answers by reference to the Term number shown in brackets at the end of each question.

73 Why do Commodity Markets or Exchanges exist and what commodities do they deal in? Name at least six. (150)

74 The Baltic Exchange is a Market. What are its functions? (151)

75 Give two other descriptions applied to Factors and Agents dealing in buying and selling goods and explain the main difference between the two. (152)

76 Which countries belong to the Group called the EEC and what do the letters CET stand for? (153–154)

77 Explain how this country's Balance of Trade figure is arrived at (a) when it is a favourable balance and (b) when it is an adverse balance. (155)

78 Explain how this country's Balance of Payments figure is arrived at. What do you understand by the terms 'favourable balance' and 'unfavourable balance'? (156)

11

Consumer Protection

Consumer Protection Terms

Term

157 Acts of Parliament

Consumers are protected under various Acts of Parliament which are amended or added to as the years pass by. The important Acts to remember are: Consumer Protection Act, Weights and Measures Acts, Sale of Goods Act, Food and Drugs Act, Trade Descriptions Act, Hire-Purchase Acts, Advertisements (Hire-Purchase) Act. (For further information on these topics look ahead to Section 15.) There are various departments and agencies to see that those acts are put into force. For example: the Department of Prices and Consumer Protection, the Office of Fair Trading, local authority Trading Standards departments and Environmental Health Officers, Consumer Advice Centres and Citizens Advice Bureaux.

158 Consumers' Association

This organization publishes *Which?* to report its comparative testing of various goods and services, the prices and charges for them, and to recommend the 'best buy'.

159 British Standards Institute (BSI)

This organization is concerned with standards for consumer goods, and the 'Kite' mark attached to an article means that it has been awarded the BSI seal of approval. BSI tests goods and inspectors visit factories to check the quality.

160 Citizens' Advice Bureaux

Most large towns have a Bureau which is a centre for free information and advice on a variety of subjects, including consumers' complaints about goods and services.

161 Industry and Trade Organizations

Such organizations test goods for their members and for the benefit of the consumer. They include the Retail Trading Standards Association (RTSA); the British Electrical Approval Board for Domestic Appliances; the Gas Council; Council of Industrial Design. Remember that apart from the Acts of Parliament which protect consumers, there are the four groups of organizations listed in Terms 158–161 which also assist the consumer.

Round 1 Questions on Consumer Protection

Check your answers by reference to the Term number shown in brackets at the end of each question.

178 Consumers are protected under various Acts of Parliament; two such Acts are ... Act and the ... Act. **(157)**

179 The Consumers' Association publishes a magazine called '...' to report their comparative testing of various ... and ... . **(158)**

180 BSI stands for ... ... and this organization's ... mark is attached to an article which has been awarded the BSI ... of ... . **(159)**

181 A large town has a C... A... B... which is a centre for free information and ... . **(160)**

182 There are Industry and Trade Organizations which test goods for their members and for the benefit of the ... . Two such Organizations are ... and ... . **(161)**

Things to do in your Research and Studies in Consumer Protection

62 Make inquiries at your local Citizens' Advice Bureau or library and obtain leaflets and booklets about consumers' rights under various Acts of Parliament. Prepare a summary of Consumers' Legal Rights.

63 Obtain copies of several *Which?* magazines and write about one or two types of goods or services reported in them.

64 Obtain some more information about the BSI.

65 Call at a Citizens' Advice Bureau with the idea of seeing for yourself what help and information are available to consumers.

66 Discuss the ways in which consumers benefit from some of the tests which one of the Industry and Trade Organizations has carried out.

Round 2 Questions on Consumer Protection

Check your answers by reference to the Term number shown in brackets at the end of each question.

79 What kinds of protection are covered by the various Acts of Parliament relating to consumers' rights? Name some of the agencies which exist to see that these acts are put into force. **(157)**

80 Explain how *Which?* and the 'Kite' mark can help to protect the consumer. **(158–159)**

81 What use is a Citizens' Advice Bureau to a consumer? **(160)**

82 Why should it be necessary for certain Trade and Industrial Organizations to test goods for their members and for the benefit of the consumer? **(161)**

12

The Stock Exchange

The Stock Exchange Terms

Term

162 Stock Exchange

This is a market place for buying and selling the shares and stock of public limited liability companies and also Government securities. The prices of these alter according to supply and demand.

163 Stock

(This must not be confused with stock-in-trade, the goods stocked by a retailer or wholesaler.) Stock Exchange stock is a share of the capital of a certain limited company; it also means a loan made to the Government for investment in Government securities such as Consolidated Stock (called 'consols') or Treasury Stock (also called gilt-edged securities).

164 Shares

These are portions of capital which shareholders own in a limited company. In exchange for the money they pay into the company, they receive share certificates and dividends on their investment out of the company's net profits. Usually, share capital is divided into shares of £1 each. If the share capital is in the form of stock, the amount can be an uneven amount (example: £100·50 of stock). In effect, shareholders own the capital of a limited company by holding shares (round figure such as £1 or 50p) or stock (odd figures such as £50·25).

165 Capital

Money or assets provided by the owner or owners of a business to run it in the hope of making a profit. Capital is used to buy assets (premises, shop-fittings, stock of goods, etc) and to cover its overheads (expenses) until they can be taken out of any profits made. (See also Simple Accounting, Section 14, page 78.)

166 Types of Shares

Public limited liability companies can issue Preference Shares.

These give a fixed rate of moderate dividend, paid to Preference shareholders before others are paid their dividends, and they receive repayment of their share capital before the other shareholders if the company goes into liquidation; Ordinary Shares (often called 'equities')—Ordinary shareholders can receive high dividends when the company's profits are high, but will receive none in bad years; Deferred Shares—no dividends are paid to owners of these shares until the other two classes of shareholders have been paid out of the company's profits. The Ordinary and Deferred shareholders have superior voting rights at company meetings over the Preference shareholders. All the foregoing types of shares can be bought and sold at the Stock Exchange. Private limited liability companies can also issue these three types of shares, but they cannot be bought and sold at the Stock Exchange. (See also Business Units, Section 13, page 74.)

167 Stockbrokers

They are Members of the Stock Exchange who deal with the public wishing to buy or sell stocks and shares. Stockbrokers go to the floor of the Stock Exchange and do business with Jobbers. When a deal has been completed, details of it are given to the buyer of the shares in the form of a Contract Note; then the seller's share certificate is sent back to the company for cancellation and replacement by a new share certificate in the name of the new shareholder.

168 Jobbers

They are Members of the Stock Exchange who deal with Stockbrokers wishing to buy or sell stocks and shares on behalf of the members of the public. Jobbers are dealers in stocks and shares on the floor of the Stock Exchange, often specializing in certain types of investment. Jobbers buy from jobbers and sell to jobbers, too. Jobbers buy at the lower of two prices and sell at the higher of two prices quoted, hoping to make a profit as commission on each deal.

169 Unit Trusts

These are organizations which appoint trustees (usually banks or insurance companies) to hold a collection of varied stocks and shares and which invite the public to buy units in the Trust. The units can be sold back to the organization at any time. Experts collect the soundest stocks and shares, collect all the dividends, deduct the Trust's expenses, and pay the rest of the dividends to the unit-holders.

170 Yield (or Return)

The percentage of dividend a buyer of shares earns on the money he has paid for them. Example: Mr A pays £200 for 100 £1 shares and the company declares a dividend of 20% on each

£1 share. The Company pays him £20; Mr A's yield is 10% on his £200 investment.

Round 1 Questions on the Stock Exchange

Check your answers by reference to the Term number shown in brackets at the end of each question.

183 The Stock Exchange is a ... ... for buying and selling ... and ... of public ... ... companies and also Government ... . **(162)**

184 Stock bought at the Stock Exchange must not be confused with ... ...-... the goods stocked by a ... or ... . **(163)**

185 Stock Exchange stock is a share of the ... you can own of a certain ... company. It also means a ... made to the Government. **(163)**

186 Shares are portions of ... which ... own in a ... . They receive share ... and ... on them out of the company's ... . **(164)**

187 Shareholders can own capital in a limited company by holding ... (round figure such as £1 or ...) or ... (odd figures such as £ ...). **(164)**

188 Capital is ... or ... provided by the owner of a business. It is used to buy ... (premises, ..., ... etc) and to cover its ... (expenses). **(165)**

189 Public limited liability companies and private limited liability companies can issue three main types of shares, namely, P... shares, O... shares and D... shares. **(166)**

190 Stockbrokers are Members of the ... ... who deal with the ... and also go to the floor of the ... ... and do business with ... . **(167)**

191 Jobbers are dealers in ... and ... on the floor of the ... . They deal with ... and with each other, buying at the ... of two prices and selling at the ... of two prices quoted. **(168)**

192 Unit Trusts are organizations which hold a collection of varied ... and ... and which invite the ... to buy ... in the T... . Experts collect the soundest ... and ..., collect all the ..., deduct expenses and pay the rest of the ... to the ...-... . **(169)**

193 Yield or Return on capital means the percentage of ... a buyer of shares earns on the money he has ... for them. **(170)**

Things to do in your Research and Studies on the Stock Exchange

67 Visit the public gallery of the Stock Exchange, see a film about the Stock Exchange, or obtain some leaflets or booklets from the Stock Exchange.

68 Make a list of some of the different types of shares listed in the financial columns of newspapers and follow their prices.

69 Study the following figures:
Mr C is a shareholder in the XYZ Company, owning 100 £1 Ordinary shares. The company declares a dividend of 20% on Ordinary shares. Mr C receives a cheque for £20 from the Company. Mr C sells his shares through his stockbroker and the Stock Exchange. Mr A buys the shares through his stockbroker and the Stock Exchange and the jobbers on both sides, paying £200 for the £100 shares. The Company declares a 20% dividend next year and sends Mr A a cheque for £20. Mr A's yield or return on his capital is 10% (20% of £200). Now calculate the dividend and yield in the following case: Mr G owns 500 £1 Ordinary shares. He receives a dividend of 10%. Mr G sells all his shares through the Stock Exchange and Mr H buys them for £400. Mr H receives a dividend of 10%. (Do not refer to these answers until you have worked out the figures independently: G's dividend = £50. H's dividend = £50; his yield = $12\frac{1}{2}$% on the £400 he paid for his £500 shares—£50 dividend divided by £400 paid, multiplied by 100 for the percentage figure = $12\frac{1}{2}$%.)

Round 2 Questions on the Stock Exchange

Check your answers by reference to the Term number shown in brackets at the end of each question.

83 Outline the procedure for buying or selling shares through the Stock Exchange. (167–168)

84 What is the meaning of 'stock' which is bought and sold on the Stock Exchange and in what way does it differ from 'shares' which are also bought and sold there. (163–164)

85 What advantages are there for the investor to become a unit-holder in a Unit Trust? (169)

86 Why is it that the yield on money paid out for shares may differ from the dividend received on them when the yield and the dividend are compared in percentage terms? (170)

13

Business Units

Business Units Terms

Term

171 Mixed Economy

The production of goods and services is carried out by both private enterprise and public enterprise (see below). 'Economy' here means the system the country runs to organize the production and distribution of the wealth people make (see also Section 8, page 50).

172 Private Enterprise

Private individuals find the capital, run the organization, take the profits, and bear the losses. Private enterprises include four main types of business unit: one-man businesses, partnerships, private limited companies, and public limited companies. (See also Sections 9, 12 and 14 for further information.)

173 One-Man Business

A private enterprise owned by one person who provides the capital, runs the business as he wishes, takes all the profits, and bears all the losses.

174 Partnership

A private enterprise owned by two or more persons (a maximum of twenty persons in most businesses). They run the business, usually according to the terms set out in their Partnership Agreement; they provide the capital on the terms agreed; they bear all the losses on the terms agreed; they share the net profits in the proportions set out in their Partnership Agreement. Some partners can have a Limited Liability, but this is unusual.

175 Private Limited Liability Company

A private enterprise owned by two or more shareholders (there can be a maximum of fifty shareholders excluding any staff who can be additional shareholders). The Company runs its business according to a set of 'rules' called the Memorandum and Articles of Association. The profits are shared among the shareholders according to the type and number of shares each owns (see

74

Term 166, page 70). Shareholders are not responsible for all the losses of a limited company—the share of loss is limited to the total amount of the shares of capital a shareholder has agreed to contribute, whether or not he has actually paid all of it. The shares cannot be sold on the Stock Exchange.

176 Public Limited Liability Company

A private enterprise owned by seven or more shareholders, the number only being limited by the number of shares. The Company runs its business according to a set of 'rules' called the Memorandum and Articles of Association. The profits are shared among the shareholders according to the type and number of shares each owns (see Term 166, page 70). As in the case of Private Companies, the shareholders' liability for the Company's losses is limited to the total amount of the shares of capital they have agreed to contribute, whether paid up or not. The shares of a Public Company are bought and sold on the Stock Exchange.

177 Public Enterprise

A general term applied to all businesses owned by the State or local authorities. For example, the State owns the Coal Board, the Gas Council, the Post Office, the Bank of England, British Rail, etc. Local authorities own libraries, local parks, public health departments, schools, etc. Any profits made by Public Enterprises belong to the people; any losses they make are borne by the people as taxpayers and ratepayers. The main reasons why some businesses are run by public enterprises and others are run by private enterprises are (a) it is more convenient or economic for a business to be controlled by a public enterprise (example, a monopoly such as the Gas Council, having sole control of North Sea gas and the distribution pipes), (b) political —some Governments favour public enterprise businesses, others favour private enterprise businesses. Our main political parties accept our present business set-up—a mixed economy—the right-wing parties stress the advantages of private enterprise; the left-wing parties favour mainly public enterprise.

178 Friendly Societies

Many non-profit-making businesses are registered with the Registrar of Friendly Societies. They include consumer organizations such as Co-operative Societies (see Term 138, page 55) and Building Societies (see Term 179 below) where excess of income over expenditure (called 'surplus') benefits the consumer.

179 Building Societies

They are friendly societies, as stated above, which enable consumers to invest their savings and also to borrow money for house-purchase through the Societies' mortgage schemes. The

Societies lend money at a higher rate of interest than the rate of interest paid to investors, the income from which being used to cover 'overheads'. A Building Society lending money is called the 'Mortgagee' (the house-buyer's creditor); the house-buyer is called the 'Mortgagor' (the Building Society's debtor). To mortgage a house means using it as a form of security in exchange for a loan; hence a Mortgage Deed is drawn up between the Building Society lending the money and the borrower of the loan. If the loan is not repaid over an agreed number of years, the Building Society can 'foreclose' and sell the borrower's house to recover what is due.

Round 1 Questions on Business Units

Check your answers by reference to the Term number shown in brackets at the end of each question.

194 The term 'mixed economy' means that the production of goods and ... is carried out by both private ... and public ... . (171)

195 Make a list of the four main types of private enterprise. (172)

196 A one-man business is a ... enterprise owned by one person who provides the ..., runs the business, takes all the ... and bears all the ... . (173)

197 From two to twenty persons (maximum of twenty in most firms) can run a ... usually under the terms set out in a ... Agreement. (174)

198 From two to fifty shareholders can run a ... enterprise called a private ... ... company. The company has a set of 'rules' called the M ... and A ... of Association. (175)

199 From seven to an unlimited number of shareholders (provided they hold shares) can run a ... enterprise called a public ... ... company. The company has a set of 'rules' called the ... and ... of ... . (176)

200 Public Enterprise is a general term applied to all businesses owned by the ... or ... . One example is ... . (177)

201 Two examples of Friendly Societies are ... ... and ... ... where excess of i ... over e ... (called 's ...') benefits the ... . (178)

202 Building Societies enable consumers to invest their ... and also to ... money for house-p ... through the Societies m ... schemes. (179)

Things to do in your Research and Studies On Business Units

70 Make three headings:
   One-Man Businesses   **Partnerships**
                Limited Companies

   and head your list **Business Units.** Write down in the correct columns as many local private enterprise businesses as possible. If a firm is named T Brown, assume it is a one-man business; if it is named Brown & Smith or Brown and Sons, assume it is a partnership; if Ltd or Limited appears at the end of its name, include it in the Companies' column (Co or Company alone at the end of a firm's name should be entered under Partnerships).

71 Head a sheet of paper **Public Enterprises** and below the heading head two columns thus:

   State Controlled   **Local Authority Controlled**

   Write down in the correct columns all the public enterprise businesses you can think of. For example, British Rail can be entered in your first column, and local public libraries in your second.

72 Find out how much interest your local building societies will pay investors and what rate of interest they charge to borrowers who wish to buy their properties on mortgage.

Round 2 Questions on Business Units

Check your answers by reference to the Term number shown in brackets at the end of each question.

87 Explain the meaning of the term 'mixed economy'. (**171**)
88 Give details of the four main types of business unit. (**172**)
89 What are the main differences between private and public limited liability companies? (**175–176**)
90 Why are some businesses run by private enterprise and others are controlled by public enterprise? (**171–172, 177**)
91 Why are building societies called 'Friendly Societies' and what are their two important functions? (**179**)

14

Simple Accounting

Simple Accounting Terms

Term

180 Capital

Capital is wealth contributed by a proprietor, partners or share-holders to a business. A firm's capital is the total of its assets (premises, motor vehicles, cash, etc) less its liabilities (bank loan, creditors, etc). Capital paid into a firm is therefore used to buy assets and to run it in order to make a profit. Borrowed capital such as a bank loan must not be included in the total capital owned by a firm (it is a liability which must be taken away from the firm's assets). (See also Section 12, The Stock Exchange, and Section 13, Business Units, for more information about this topic.)

181 Assets

Items owned by a business such as cash, stock-in-trade, shop-fittings and shop-premises.

182 Liabilities

Debts owing by a business such as a bank overdraft, a bank loan, creditors (money owing to suppliers of goods, etc) and unpaid wages.

183 Gross Profit

The difference between a firm's total net sales and the net cost of the goods sold (called purchases). Example: Net Sales = £5,000; Net Purchases less goods unsold = £4,000; Gross Profit = £1,000. If the cost of the goods sold had been £5,500, the firm would have made a **Gross Loss** of £500.

184 Overheads

These are a firm's expenses in running the business. Examples: wages, rent, heating and lighting, repairs, etc. They are also called revenue expenses as they are deducted from a firm's revenue (income) to calculate the net profit.

185 Net Profit

The difference between a firm's gross profit and the overheads.

Example: Gross Profit (as shown in Term 183) £1,000; Overheads £600; Net Profit = £400, which is the owner's return on the capital he has put into his business. (Look at Terms 172 to 176 on pages 74 and 75 for further information about Net Profit.)

186 Stock-Taking and Turnover

The stock of goods unsold (called 'stock-in-hand' or 'stock-in-trade') is priced at cost price or the current market price, whichever is the lower. Stock-in-hand is one of the assets of a firm (see Term 181, page 78). It is deducted from a firm's purchases when arriving at the figure for the cost of goods sold (see Term 183, page 78).

The total net sales of a company is called its *turnover*. The *rate of turnover* is the number of times that the average value of stock for a given period is sold in that period. There are two ways of calculating the rate of turnover.

(1) Divide the production cost of sales by the average production cost of stock.

(2) Divide turnover by the average value of stock at selling price.

187 Trade Discount

This is an allowance deducted from a seller's invoice to enable the purchaser to make a gross profit when the latter sells the goods. It is the difference between the wholesale and the retail price. (For further information look at Section 4 and Term 81, page 27.)

188 Cash Discount

This is an additional allowance made by the seller to the purchaser of goods to encourage the latter to settle the invoice within a certain period, usually one month from the purchase date. (Look at Section 4 again and Term 81, page 27, for further information on this topic.)

189 Balance Sheet

This is a firm's financial statement showing items it owns (called Assets) on one side of the account, and items it owes (called Liabilities) on the other side, and the difference between the two totals on the Liabilities side called Capital (wealth due to the owner)—both sides must be equal in total. (See also Terms 180, 181 and 182, page 78.)

Round 1 Questions on Simple Accounting Terms

Check your answers by reference to the Term number shown in brackets at the end of each question.

203 Capital is ... contributed by a person to a business. A firm's capital is the total of its ... less its ... . **(180)**

204 Capital paid into a firm is used to buy ... and to run it in order to make a .... **(180)**

205 Items owned by a business such as cash and premises are called .... **(181)**

206 Debts owing by a business such as bank loans and bank overdrafts are called .... **(182)**

207 Gross profit is the difference between net ... and the net cost of the ... ... (called ...) . **(183)**

208 The opposite to a gross profit is a ... . **(183)**

209 A firm's running expenses are called .... . Examples of these are wages, rent and .... **(184)**

210 Net profit is the difference between a firm's gross ... and the .... The total net sales of a firm is called .... The number of times the average stock is sold in a particular period of time is called the ... of .... **(185–186)**

211 In stock-taking, the stock-in- ... is priced at ... ... or the current ... price, whichever is the .... **(186)**

212 Trade discount is an ... deducted from a seller's ... to enable the purchaser to make a ... . **(187)**

213 Cash discount is an additional ... to encourage the ... to settle the ... within a certain period. **(188)**

214 A balance sheet is a firm's financial ... showing items it owns (called ...) on one side and items it owes (called ...) on the other side plus the balance called ... —both sides must be .... **(189)**

Things to do in your Research and Studies on Simple Accounting Terms

73 Write down the following figures and find out (a) the Gross Profit, (b) the Net Profit, (c) the increased Capital after adding to it the Net Profit, (d) the total of the left-hand side of the Balance Sheet, (e) the total of the right-hand side of the Balance Sheet:

Net Sales £10,000; Cost of the Goods sold £7,000; Overheads £1,000; Capital contributed by the owner £8,000; Bank Loan £500; Creditors £1,500; Shop Premises £6,000; Stock-in-Hand £1,000; Debtors (people owing money to the firm) £1,000; Shop Fittings £2,000; Motor Van £1,800; Cash £200. Set out your work as under:

Sales	£			
Cost of Goods	£			
Gross Profit	£			
Overheads	£			
Net Profit	£			

Capital	£	Shop Premises	£	
add Net Profit	£	Shop Fittings	£	
Present Capital	£	Motor Van	£	
Bank Loan	£	Stock-in-Hand	£	
Creditors	£	Debtors	£	
		Cash in Hand	£	
	£		£	

(After completing your work, check your answers with these figures: Gross Profit £3,000; Net Profit £2,000; Present Capital £10,000; Total Liabilities side (left-hand side) £12,000; Total Assets (right-hand side) £12,000.)

74 Selling price of goods shown in invoice £20,000; trade discount deducted = 20%; work out the net amount of the invoice; the retailer settles the bill within a month and earns 10% cash discount: how much does he pay the wholesaler? (Answers check: TD £4,000; invoice total £16,000; CD £1,600; retailer pays £14,400.)

Round 2 Questions on Simple Accounting Terms

Check your answers by reference to the Term number shown in brackets at the end of each question.

92 Explain the meaning of the terms 'capital', 'assets', 'liabilities'. (180–182)
93 Explain the terms 'gross profit', 'net profit', 'overheads', 'turnover', 'rate of turnover'. (183–186)
94 What is the difference between 'cash discount' and 'trade discount'? (187–188)
95 What is a 'balance sheet' and what information appears in it? (189)

15

Cash, Credit, Rental and Hire Transactions

Cash, Credit, Rental and Hire Transactions Terms

Term

190 Cash Purchases

The term applies to goods bought and paid for at the point of sale. Actual cash, cheque, postal order, money order, bank card, etc, can be used for the purchase of goods.

191 Credit Purchases and Credit

Credit purchases are goods bought and taken away without immediate payment being made. The goods then belong to the purchaser even though he has not paid for them. The term 'credit' means that goods, property, assets or services may be purchased and payment deferred.

Some advantages of credit: People with little wealth or limited incomes can buy a house through a mortgage scheme (see Term 179); businesses can extend their trade by borrowing money (see Terms 3, 4, 27 and Term 192); goods, services and assets can be bought on credit (see Term 81, and Terms 180–181); people can buy goods and services on the spot by using credit cards and cheque cards (see Terms 28–29 and Terms 192–194) or buy on hire purchase if they take up the 'option to buy' the goods they hire (see Term 195). Credit increases the demand for goods and services, thus increasing business sales, reducing unemployment and increasing many workers' standards of living.

Some disadvantages of credit: People and businesses usually pay extra for goods, services, property and assets if payment is deferred and in the case of hire purchase, they cannot own the item until the final instalment has been paid; interest is paid on borrowed money; the advantage of cash discounts on some cash sales is lost; heavy debts can be run up, sometimes leading to insolvency (bankruptcy—unable to pay debts); people can be more easily influenced by advertisements to buy (see Term 112).

192 Extended Credit (also called Deferred Payment or Credit Sale)

The purchaser pays an initial payment or deposit and takes away the goods. He pays the rest of the cost monthly and is usually charged a small credit charge. He owns the goods from the beginning.

193 Budget Account

There are various types of budget account. Usually, the customer chooses the goods, pays a deposit, gives references, and is later given an account card; he takes other goods away from time to time, which are charged to his account and card; he takes in his card when paying the retailer any amounts off his debt which must not exceed an agreed sum. The customer is charged a small sum for buying goods on this credit basis. The goods belong to him immediately.

194 Ordinary Monthly Account

An arrangement under which a customer takes the goods away, pays the account within a month but does not receive any cash discount and the retailer does not charge for waiting for his money.

195 Hire-Purchase

The customer hires the goods and they belong to the retailer until all the agreed monthly payments have been paid; then the hirer has the 'option to buy' the goods and the retailer must by law agree to sell them to him on the payment of a further small sum (called a 'nominal sum'). The consumer is protected by the Hire-purchase Acts. (For further information see Section 11, Consumer Protection and Term 157, page 68.)

196 Rental and Hire Transactions

Rental is the term applied to the charge made by the owner of goods or property to a person wishing to use the rented goods, house, etc. The ownership remains in the hands of the owner unless agreement is made to alter the arrangement. Hire is a similar term to 'rental' and the conditions of ownership are the same. The term 'hire' is often applied to goods or property borrowed for a short period—example: we hire a car for a day but rent a house for a longer period.

Round 1 Questions on Cash, Credit, Rental and Hire Transactions

Check your answers by reference to the Term number shown in brackets at the end of each question.

215 The term 'cash purchase' applies to all goods bought for actual ... or by ..., postal order, ... order, bank card, etc. **(190)**

216 When goods are bought and taken away without immediate payment being made a ...... has taken place and the goods then belong to the .... **(191)**

217 Extended credit is also called '.........'. The purchaser pays a ..., takes away the goods, pays the balance ..., usually pays a small ...... and owns the ... from the beginning. **(192)**

218 Usually, a customer having a budget account chooses the goods, pays a ..., gives ..., and is then given an ... card. He can purchase goods from time to time which are charged to his ... and .... His debt must not exceed an ... sum. The goods belong immediately to .... **(193)**

219 An ordinary monthly account is an arrangement under which a customer takes away the goods, pays the ... within a ... without receiving any ...... and the retailer does not charge for waiting for his .... **(194)**

220 Under a hire-purchase agreement a customer ... the goods and they belong to the ... until all the agreed ...... have been paid; then the hirer has the '... to ...' . **(195)**

221 Rental is the ... made by the owner of goods or property and ... remains in his hands unless agreed to otherwise. Hire is the term often applied to goods or property ... for a ... period. Example: we ... a car for a day but ... a house for a longer period. **(196)**

Things to do in your Research and Studies in connection with Cash, Credit, Rental and Hire Transactions

75 Make inquiries about the purchase of an expensive item such as a colour television set or a suite of furniture with a view to comparing prices:

		Total cost
(a)	Cash Price, noting any cash discount allowed	£
(b)	Ordinary Monthly Account	£
(c)	Credit Purchase, payment to be made within a week or two	£
(d)	Extended Credit, noting the deposit, the credit charge and the monthly payments	£
(e)	Budget Account, noting the deposit, the credit charge, the monthly payments, and the peak figure of indebtedness allowed	£
(f)	The total monthly payments including any deposit, and the nominal sum payable to own the goods at the end of the Hire Purchase agreement	£

(e) Rental or hire charge per annum, to compare
   the cost of ownership of the goods with renting
   or hiring them   £

76 Obtain leaflets and booklets relating to credit purchase, hire-
   purchase, and renting or hiring goods.

Round 2 Questions on Cash, Credit, Rental and Hire Transactions

Check your answers by reference to the Term number shown in
brackets at the end of each question.

96 What does the term 'cash purchase' mean? What other means
   are available to customers who wish to own goods immediately
   but cannot offer full payment for them at the same time?
   (190–194)
97 Explain the main differences between budget accounts and
   ordinary monthly accounts for credit purchases. **(193–194)**
98 Outline some of the main differences between obtaining goods
   on a hire-purchase basis and renting them. **(195–196)**

Revision Tests

Each test is made up of fifteen Round 1 Questions and the Round Two Questions.

The question numbers in each of the fifteen tests below refer to Round 1 Questions throughout the book. In the case of questions with missing words, write down only the missing words.

Marks for Round 1 Questions = 5 per answer = 75 marks
                Round 2 Questions = 25 per answer = 25 Marks   100 marks

Round 1 Questions

(Answer all the Round 1 Questions numbered in each Test)

Test 1	1	31	54	69	89	113	123	129	140	165	177	182	193	202	214
Test 2	2	32	55	70	90	114	124	130	141	166	178	183	194	203	215
Test 3	3	33	56	71	91	115	125	131	142	167	179	184	195	204	216
Test 4	4	34	57	72	92	116	126	132	143	168	180	185	196	205	217
Test 5	5	35	58	73	93	117	127	133	144	169	181	186	197	206	218
Test 6	6	36	59	74	94	118	128	134	145	170	23	187	198	207	219
Test 7	7	37	60	75	95	119	51	135	146	171	24	188	199	208	220
Test 8	8	38	61	76	96	120	52	136	147	172	25	189	200	209	159
Test 9	9	39	62	77	97	121	53	137	148	173	26	190	201	210	160
Test 10	10	40	63	78	98	122	69	138	149	174	27	191	108	211	161
Test 11	11	41	64	79	99	46	70	139	150	175	28	192	109	212	162
Test 12	12	42	65	80	100	47	71	16	151	176	29	104	110	213	163
Test 13	13	43	66	81	101	48	84	17	152	20	30	105	111	156	164
Test 14	14	44	67	82	102	49	85	18	153	21	87	106	112	157	221
Test 15	15	45	68	83	103	50	86	19	154	22	88	107	155	158	31

Round 2 Questions

The question numbers in each of the fifteen tests below refer to Round 2 Questions throughout the book. Choose only **ONE** question in each test.

Test 1	1	13	19	25	32	44	52
Test 2	2	14	20	26	33	45	53
Test 3	3	15	21	27	34	46	54
Test 4	4	16	22	28	35	47	55
Test 5	5	17	23	29	36	48	56
Test 6	6	18	24	30	37	49	57
Test 7	7	58	62	31	38	50	72
Test 8	8	59	63	78	39	51	73
Test 9	9	60	64	79	40	82	74
Test 10	10	61	65	80	41	83	75
Test 11	11	86	66	81	42	84	76
Test 12	12	87	67	91	43	85	77
Test 13	95	88	68	92	94	1	31
Test 14	96	89	69	93	98	69	89
Test 15	97	90	70	71	3	32	55

Round 3 Questions—a Series of Examination Papers based on the Commerce Terms in this Textbook

Notes on Round 3 Questions

The Round 3 Questions are grouped together to form Examination Papers. Each Paper contains thirteen short-answer questions and 1 essay-type answer question; the latter can be chosen from two alternatives. The time allowed has been confined to 30 minutes to enable the Examinations to take place in normal lesson times.

Additional Round 3 Examinations Papers can be prepared from the Terms Index and the Round 2 Questions in this textbook. Reference to the Rounds 1 and 2 Questions Revision Tests should be useful in compiling those additional Papers.

Commerce Examination 1
(Time allowed—30 minutes)

Answers should not be written in this book.

Part I (Answer all the questions)

Choose the correct word or phrase to complete the sentence:

1 Banking is part of a section of Commerce called

  Trade   Industry   Commercial Services
     Direct Services   Production   (3 marks)

2 The insurance contract which sets out the terms and conditions of insurance cover is known as the
        Premium   Cover Note   Quotation
        Statement of Account   Policy   (3 marks)

Complete questions 3 and 4 by choosing the correct term for each sentence from the following list of terms (some of the terms are unwanted ones):

Deposit account
Budget account
Premium Bonds

British Bonds
Current account
Savings account
Monthly account

3 Cheques are drawn on a customer's ... . (3 marks)
4 No interest is paid on Post Office ... . (3 marks)

Complete questions 5–8.

5 A ... ... sets out the total of each bill sent to a purchaser of goods, plus any amount owing by him at the end of the previous month, less any allowances made by him and any cash he has paid to the seller, and a final figure representing the balance the purchaser owes to the seller at the end of the month. (3 marks)

6 Customs Officers supervise dutiable goods which are discharged from a ship and placed in a ... . (3 marks)

7 People who produce goods and services are classified under the three branches of production, namely, ... , ... , ... (3 marks)

8 There are many types of retailer, one type being multiple shops. Three other types of retailer are ... ... , and ... . (3 marks)

9 State two advantages of using road transport for conveying goods. (2 marks)

10 State two advantages of having wholesalers involved in the distribution of goods. (2 marks)

11 Name one advantage and one disadvantage of advertising. (2 marks)

12 Study the five terms and then answer the questions: partnership, one-man business, public limited company, public enterprise and private limited company.
Which one is the odd one out?
Why is it the odd one out?
What is common to the other four? (1 + 2 + 2 marks)

13 Study the five terms and then answer the questions: delivery note, advice note, consignment note, cover note and credit note.
Which one is the odd one out?
Why is it the odd one out?
What is common to the other four? (1 + 2 + 2 marks)

Part II (Answer ONE of the three questions)

14 What are the differences between the ownership and management of a co-operative retail society and a private enterprise department store? (10 marks)

15 Describe the two Post Office services relating to mail which is retained for collection by an addressee. (10 marks)

16 Compare the investment of savings in (a) Post Office Savings schemes and (b) Company shares. (10 marks)

(TOTAL 50 marks)

Commerce Examination 2

(Time allowed—30 minutes)

Answers should not be written in this book.

Part I (Answer all the questions)

Choose the correct word or phrase to complete the sentence.

1 The bill which is sent by the seller to the buyer containing details of the goods, their quantities and prices, and other relevant details relating to a credit purchase is termed:

order   advice note   price list
invoice   quotation   (3 marks)

2 The safest form of cheque is:

a cheque with a general crossing   a post-dated cheque   an open cheque   a cheque with a special crossing   a stale cheque   (3 marks)

Choose the correct term for each of the two sentences below from the following list of terms (some of the terms are unwanted):

extractive industry   manufacturing industry
service industry   trade
commercial service   direct service

3 The work of a dustman is classified as ... . (3 marks)

4 The work of a farmer or his staff is classified as ... . (3 marks)

Complete the following sentences:

5 The ... ... is a market for buying and selling shipping and air space for imports and exports. (3 marks)

6 Stall-holders often sell their goods to consumers in the ... . (3 marks)

7 Three main classes of shares which are issued by limited liability companies are:
... ..., ..., and ... . (3 marks)

Complete the following sentence:

8 The three main kinds of credit accounts made available by retailers are: ..., ..., and ... . (3 marks)
9 Name two examples of mass media advertising. (2 marks)
10 Give two reasons for having a warehouse. (2 marks)
11 Name two types of business unit. (2 marks)
12 Study the five terms below and then answer the questions:
cash, stock-in-trade, bank loan, motor van, premises.
Which is the odd one out?
Why is it the odd one out?
What is common to the other four? (1 + 2 + 2 marks)

13 Study the five terms below and then answer the questions:
BSI, COD, KITE, *Which?*, RTSA.
Which is the odd one out?
Why is it the odd one out?
What is common to the other four? (1 + 2 + 2 marks)

Part II (Answer **ONE** of the three questions)

14 Compare the Recorded Delivery service and the Registration service which are provided by the Post Office. (10 marks)
OR
15 Name the three types of insurance cover which should be taken out by a business-man and give reasons for your choice. (10 marks)
OR
16 A manufacturer and a wholesaler both have rail sidings at their premises. Discuss the question of using rail transport or road transport for the despatch of goods from the factory to the warehouse, giving advantages of both methods. (10 marks)

(TOTAL 50 marks)

Commerce Examination 3

(Time allowed–30 minutes)

Answers should not be written in this book.

Part I (Answer all the questions)

Choose the correct word or phrase to complete the sentence.

1 The quickest type of transport to use for the conveyance of a letter from London to Cardiff would be by (choose from the five):

coastal steamer   express freight train

taxi   Railex   hovercraft   (3 marks)

2 The maximum amount of compensation for loss in transit is payable by the Post Office service called:

recorded delivery   advice of delivery

registration   certificate of posting

business reply   (3 marks)

Complete questions 3 and 4 by choosing the correct term for each sentence from the following list of terms (some of the terms are unwanted).

renewal notice   cover note   policy

proposal form   contract   premium

3 In order to keep an insurance policy 'alive', the insured must pay the annual ... on time.   (3 marks)

4 The insurance ... is the contract which the insurer sends to the insured.   (3 marks)

Complete the following sentences:

5 The abbreviation **EEC** stands for ... ...   (3 marks)
6 The abbreviation **COD** stands for ... ...   (3 marks)

Read the following two paragraphs carefully and then complete the sentences by filling in the missing word or words.

7 When a customer opens a current account with a bank he receives a ... ... for crediting his account and a ... ... for debiting his account and the bank will send him from time to time a ... ... setting out the credits and debits and the current balances.   (3 marks)

8 If a seller overcharges a customer he may send him a ... ... but if he undercharges him he may send the customer a ... . At the end of the month the customer will receive a ... ...   (3 marks)

9 Name the two groups of Members of the Stock Exchange who meet there on the floor of the Exchange to buy and sell stocks and shares. (2 marks)

10 The difference between a firm's total net sales and the cost of the goods sold and the balance remaining after the deduction of overheads from that difference have special accounting terms. Name the two terms. (2 marks)

11 Two motives to which advertisers appeal are ... and ... . (2 marks)

12 Study the five terms below and then answer the questions:
bank clerk, insurance agent, warehouseman, train-driver, teacher.
Which is the odd one out?
Why is it the odd one out?
What is common to the other four? (1 + 2 + 2 = 5 marks)

13 Study the five terms below and then answer the questions:
Great Britain, West Germany, France, Egypt and Denmark.
Which is the odd one out?
Why is it the odd one out?
What is common to the other four? (1 + 2 + 2 = 5 marks)

Part II (Answer **ONE** of the three questions)

14 Write about two advertisements you have seen and comment on the advantages gained by those who buy and sell the products advertised. (10 marks)
OR
15 Today's consumer is protected in many ways and he can seek advice about the goods and services which he may wish to obtain. Discuss. (10 marks)
OR
16 Why is it essential for a business-man to have a banking account and what other banking services are available to him? (10 marks)

(TOTAL 50 marks)

Terms Index

94

95